BASEBALL'S WACKY PLAYERS

George Sullivan

Illustrated with photographs

DODD, MEAD & COMPANY
New York

PICTURE CREDITS

AP/Wide World Photos, 29, 31; Atlanta Braves, 47; Baseball Hall of Fame, 124, 136; Baseball Nostalgia, 109, 133, 140; Boston Red Sox, 51; Chicago Cubs (Stephen Green), 37, 40; Detroit Tigers, 63, 64, 69, 71, 89; Houston Astros, 44; New York Yankees, 106; Pawtucket Red Sox, 78; St. Louis Cardinals, 48; Seattle Mariners, 58; Texas Rangers, 27; Copyright Topps Chewing Gum, Inc., 90, 91, 92, 93, 94; United Press International, 10, 15, 18, 23, 35, 46, 56, 99, 114, 117, 120, 129. All other photographs are by George Sullivan.

1   2   3   4   5   6   7   8   9   10

Library of Congress Cataloging in Publication Data

Sullivan, George, date
  Baseball's wacky players.

  Includes index.
  Summary: Accounts of antics by some of baseball's
most colorful players.
  1. Baseball players—United States—Biography—
Juvenile literature.   2. Practical jokes—Juvenile
literature.   [1. Baseball players.   2. Practical
jokes]   I. Title.
GV865.A1585   1984   796.357'092'2 [B]   84-13590
ISBN 0-396-08459-1

Acknowledgments

Many people contributed in the preparation of this book. Special thanks are due Dan Ewald, Detroit Tigers; Chuck Adams, Office of the Baseball Commissioner; Bob Korch, Atlanta Braves; Norman J. Liss, Liss Public Relations; Joe Safety, New York Yankees; Steve Brill, WISN, Milwaukee; Clarke Ickes, Baltimore *News-American;* Bob DiBiaso, Cleveland Indians; Jay Horwitz, New York Mets; Josh Spofford, Boston Red Sox; Stephen Green, Chicago Cubs; Ralph Nozaki, *The Mistake Manual;* Francesca Kurti, TLC Custom Labs; Tim Mead, Atlanta Braves; Mike Tamburra, Pawtucket Red Sox; Jim Benagh; and John Devaney.

Contents

①

Wild and Crazy Guys

Just a few seasons ago, 25-year-old Joe Charboneau was the talk of the Cleveland Indians. He was Super Joe, 6-foot-2, 200 pounds, with a broad chest and shoulders. The fans loved him. He was always patient with autograph seekers. And he'd throw balls into the stands to screaming kids.

Charboneau was not even supposed to make the team in 1980. But in his second appearance at the plate in a Cleveland uniform, he belted a home run. And in his first home game, he went 3-for-3, topping off the performance with another homer.

Charboneau ended up with 87 runs batted in and 23 home runs. He walked off with American League Rookie of the Year honors.

Not only did Charboneau carry a big bat, but he entertained his friends and teammates with his bizarre behavior. He ate the rawhide covers off of baseballs. He drank beer through his nose. He once brought home a baby alligator to raise.

Joe Charboneau, a superslugger, a free spirit

About the craziest thing that Charboneau ever did was to eat six lighted cigarettes. "It was at a party," he said. "The trick is to swallow 'em fast, but make sure you have plenty of saliva before you try it."

Another time, to win a bet, Charboneau swallowed a raw egg whole, shell and all. "It got stuck in my throat and I started choking," he recalled. "A friend hauled off and punched me in the Adam's apple. It smashed the egg and it went right down."

Joe Charboneau seemed too good to be true. He had an explosive swing. He had a fierce desire to succeed. And there was that zany side to him, which delighted the fans and the media.

His biography became a best seller in Cleveland. A rock band hailed his talents in the song "Go, Go, Joe Charboneau." "He lit up the city," said Bert Graeff, a baseball writer for the Cleveland *Press*.

A brilliant career was forecast for Charboneau. "Joe could have a great future," said Toby Harrah, a veteran outfielder and one of Charboneau's closest friends on the Indians. "The only thing that worries me is his capacity to destroy himself."

Harrah's worry was no idle one. At spring training in 1981, Charboneau injured his back sliding into second base. Despite enormous pain, he continued to play. But he was no longer a feared slugger. Midway through the season, Cleveland sent him to the Charleston Charlies of the Class AAA International League. With Charleston, Charboneau hit .217 in 14 games. "I went from the Hall of Fame to the Hall of Shame," he said.

With the season over, Charboneau underwent surgery to repair the damage to his back. His comeback attempt the next season failed.

In the spring of 1982, Charboneau showed up at spring training with a spray-painted punk haircut. He seemed to have lost his confidence and was said to be experimenting too much with his batting style. He was sent back to Charleston, where he struggled. Later that season, he was demoted to the Chattanooga Lookouts of the Class AA Southern League.

Charboneau tried to come back again in 1983. By June, he was batting .200 for the Buffalo Bisons, an Indian farm team in the Class AA Eastern League. Cleveland decided to put an end to the baseball saga of Joe Charboneau and handed him his release.

Joe Charboneau is remembered here because he was one of

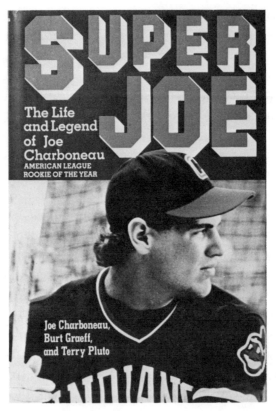

Charboneau's biography was a best seller in Cleveland.

the most free-thinking, free-spirited baseball clowns of recent years. He was, in a word, a flake.

A flake is many things. Odd. Unpredictable. Weird. Off-the-wall.

According to Randy Youngman of the Baltimore *News-American,* Jackie Brandt, an outfielder and occasional infielder for six major league teams during an eleven-year career, was the first player to whom the term "flake" was applied. When Brandt was a rookie with the St. Louis Browns in 1956, a teammate once commented that "things seemed to flake off his mind and disappear."

Brandt once played 27 holes of golf in 101-degree heat before a doubleheader. Now, that's flaky. Brandt went 7-for-10 that day. "I took a five-minute nap before going to the ball park," he explained.

"I don't know why the newspapermen call me Jackie," Brandt once said. "I prefer Jack and my friends call me Flaky." Even my two-year-old calls me Flaky, not Da-da."

Baseball has always had its share of flakes. Sometimes they are called nuts or screwballs.

Sparky Lyle, who won fame as a relief pitcher for the New York Yankees during the late 1970s and was later traded to the Texas Rangers, was a noted flake. Before a night game at Arlington Stadium not long ago, Lyle turned in one of baseball's zaniest performances of the 1980s. Lyle was out in right field, when he began to be pestered for a baseball by several hundred Little League fans who were seated in a group in the bleachers. Lyle tossed a ball into the stands.

The kids clamored for more. Lyle took off his cap and threw it into the stands.

The kids wanted more. Lyle removed his jersey and threw it into the stands.

More kids had joined the group by now. The yelling was louder. Lyle took off his shoes and socks and threw them into the stands.

The kids wanted more. Lyle threw his baseball glove into the stands.

The kids begged for more. Lyle took off his pants and threw them into the stands.

13

Standing in his underwear, Lyle put his hand on his hips and looked up into the stands. The screaming was at a fever pitch.

Sparky decided it was time to end the show. He disappeared into the clubhouse to get dressed again.

There is probably more zaniness in baseball than in any other sport. Much of it arises out of the tedium the players must endure. Baseball is frequently a boring profession. Sure, there are those crucial games played before screaming fans in packed stadiums, but such games are relatively rare. A professional baseball player spends much of his time waiting. Once he awakens and has his first meal of the day, he waits for the bus to arrive to take him to the stadium. Then he waits for the game to begin. After, he boards the team bus again for the return trip to the hotel, or perhaps to the airport. There he and his teammates wait to board their plane. Each day is two or three hours of baseball; much of the rest is waiting.

John Lowenstein of the Baltimore Orioles once said his status in baseball reminded him of the characters in a play by Samuel Beckett titled *Waiting for Godot*. The play tells of two men who spend their lives waiting for someone they know who will never show up. They realize it is futile, but they continue to wait and wait.

"Baseball is a lot like that," Lowenstein said. "We do the same thing every day. The games are the same. Only the results are different."

In Beckett's play, the characters joke to keep their sanity. Baseball players do the same.

Baseball nuttiness also has to be inspired by the uniforms players wear. After all, it is not easy to represent yourself as a

Relief pitcher Lyle remained in character by wearing a fireman's helmet to his wedding.

serious person when you are wearing knickers. Imagine Howard Cosell in a baseball uniform. Or Teddy Kennedy. It makes you grin to think of it.

Granted, today's uniforms are not knickers of the classic type. Tight, tapered uniforms are the style today. These go back to 1960, when Willie Mays began having his loose-fitting uniforms carefully tailored to suit his personal taste.

A decade later, the Pittsburgh Pirates institutionalized the change when they introduced glove-tight, double-knit uniforms. Some players say the uniform today makes you look like you're wearing ski pants. Others say long johns. Either way, the uniform does seem to encourage the idea of having fun.

More than a few players can say that boredom is not a problem for them; tension is, and they clown around to keep relaxed. Some claim that their antics help to keep the entire ball club loose.

There's no doubt that flaky conduct can be helpful in relieving tension. In a game played at Yankee Stadium several years ago, New York relief pitcher Goose Gossage was having a rough day. No matter what he threw, opposing batters kept blasting his pitches to the deepest reaches of the outfield. Time after time, center fielder Mickey Rivers had to race to the wall to haul down the ball.

After returning to his position after yet another trek to the fence, Rivers decided it was time to send a message to Gossage. Rivers turned his back on the infield and dropped down into the starting position for a sprinter, putting both hands to the ground in front of him and positioning his feet for a quick getaway.

When Gossage turned and noticed Rivers, he broke up, laughing aloud on the mound. The tension broken, Gossage quickly retired the side.

Another time Rivers strapped a catcher's chest protector to his back and walked around the clubhouse wearing it. He explained to his teammates that he planned to wear it during the game to protect him as he ran for the wall chasing the missiles that were hit off the pitching of Catfish Hunter. Hunter, one of the most popular of the Yankees, took the ribbing good-naturedly.

Occasionally a player will aim his humor at himself. In the 1981 World Series, New York vs. Los Angeles, Yankee star Dave Winfield, who had recently been dubbed the $26 million man because of the big contract he had signed, went to bat sixteen consecutive times without collecting a base hit. After he finally managed a weak single, he stood at first base and asked for the ball as a souvenir. He was kidding, of course. He simply realized that he had been a major disappointment in the series. By poking fun at himself and his puny hit, he was easing the pressure, and perhaps paving the way for some run-producing slugging.

The Baltimore Orioles of the late 1970s and early 1980s were a loose team. Also a winning team. The players developed a wide variety of amusing rituals.

Ten minutes before every game, pitcher Don Stanhouse would emit a high-pitched, blood-curdling scream. In the dugout, Lee May would stage a mock argument with a teammate, and they would holler at the top of their lungs at each other until everyone else was laughing. Ken Singleton would lead a locomotive cheer for Al Bumbry as he entered the batter's box as the lead-off hitter. As pitcher Steve Stone once noted, "This is a 'we' team, not an 'I' team." Such antics were credited with playing an important role in helping the Orioles win the American League championship and defeat the Phillies in the World Series in 1983.

Sad to say, the free spirit, the goofball, the flake is much less a part of baseball than used to be the case. Whereas a team nowadays might have one or two flaky characters, in days past craziness was widespread. And it wasn't just the fringe players that clowned around; the star players did, too. Willie Mays, Mickey Mantle, Hank Aaron, and Warren Spahn got as many laughs out of the game as anyone.

Why were players of the past more colorful?

Many reasons. Money is one. Players used to receive salaries that were about the same as those of the average worker. Not anymore. Nowadays, superstars are paid a million dollars a year and more. Even second-string players and bench warmers receive

Jay Johnstone played a flake's role on eight different teams in a career that began in the late 1960s and stretched into the 1980s.

amounts that were undreamed-of less than a generation ago. Dugout conversations used to concern baseball, and only baseball. Now such topics as investments and tax shelters are discussed. For many players, *The Wall Street Journal* has replaced *The Sporting News* as preferred reading matter.

Tim McCarver, a National League catcher during the 1960s and 1970s, and later a broadcaster for the New York Mets, has noted that players today don't stick around the clubhouse after a game and talk baseball like they once did. "When the game is over, they scatter," he says. "They've got other commitments, business meetings and such."

With players being paid so much, they're much more serious about the game. They keep themselves in better shape than players of a generation ago. They are also much more likely to stick to the straight and narrow as far as their conduct is concerned.

"There are fewer colorful individuals today," Bill Veeck, a club owner who always made an effort to entertain the fans, said not long ago in an article in the Baltimore *News-American*. "There aren't as many free spirits."

Veeck remembers Jackie Price, a minor league shortstop, "who could play catch and hit while standing on his head." He remembers Rabbit Maranville, "who did handsprings and flips on the base paths," and infielder Cuckoo Christensen, "who played the outfield with a newspaper. He would poke holes in it so he could see. He also caught pop-ups in his pocket."

"You don't find individuals like that anymore," said Veeck.

Veeck might also have cited Ossie Schreckengost, a catcher with the Cleveland Indians in the early 1900s. During spring training one season, Schreckengost and his teammates were lodged in a New Orleans hotel not noted for the quality of its food. For

19

one thing, the steaks were always tough. After wrestling with them for a time, the players would frequently order the waiters to take the steaks back to the kitchen. But this didn't solve the problem, for the same steaks would just be reheated and served again.

Then the players got the idea of carving their initials into the steaks. This, they figured, would enable them to recognize when a steak was making a return appearance.

One day, Schreckengost, after struggling with a steak for several minutes, flipped it over to find that it bore three sets of initials. Without a word, he got up from the table, carried the steak to the cashier's desk, and angrily demanded a hammer. When one was provided, Schreckengost took the steak and nailed it to the dining room door while the guests looked on in shock.

Not many players today would do what Ossie Schreckengost did. Nevertheless, there are still plenty of wild and crazy players on the loose. Their hotdogging, sick humor, and clubhouse pranks are an important part of modern baseball. While baseball is changing all the time, wackiness, like nine innings to a game and three strikes you're out, has been a constant for more than a century.

②

Superflakes

Just about every major league baseball team has at least one flaky character. Those that don't wish they did. No clubhouse is fun without one. Rides on the team bus are dull and uneventful.

Who are baseball's wacky players? What makes them flaky?

Three of the most noted flakes of recent years are profiled in this chapter. They are: Doug Rader, who spent more than a decade playing third base for Houston, San Diego, and Toronto before becoming manager of the Texas Rangers in 1983; John Lowenstein, or Big Lo or Steiner, as he was called by his teammates on the Baltimore Orioles, where his flakiness came to national attention when the Orioles won the World Series in 1983; and Jay Johnstone, a flake with eight different teams in a career that spanned more than fifteen seasons.

Ex-Yankee Jim Bouton, author of *Ball Four*, once interviewed Doug Rader for a television program. Rader was leaning on a rake, with which he periodically scratched his face.

"How did you happen to become a ballplayer?" Bouton asked.

"It was my environment," said Rader. "When you're stealing hubcaps and spending a lot of time in jail, you can't help but become a ballplayer."

"Do you have any advice for Little Leaguers?" Bouton continued, struggling to keep a straight face.

"They should chew the gum that comes with the baseball cards," Rader said, "and they should also eat the cards. Bubble gum cards are very good in a Little Leaguer's diet."

"Just any bubble gum cards?" Bouton asked.

"No," said Rader. "They should only eat the cards of good ballplayers. You don't want them digesting bad statistics that would hurt them.

"Say you got a kid who's 5-foot-1. Let him eat a Willie McCovey card. Willie is 6-foot-4. The kid may grow. You can never tell."

You could never tell about Doug Rader, either.

Rader was Houston's third baseman for nine years, then spent a couple of seasons with San Diego and Toronto. (He was named to manage the Texas Rangers in 1983.) He was nicknamed the Red Rooster for his fiery temperament and his strutting, headfirst style of play.

He stood 6-foot-3; he weighed 220. For a big man, he was remarkably agile and quick. A shock of brownish-red hair usually protruded from the back of his cap. His Astro teammates said he looked like the cartoon character Foghorn Leghorn.

He certainly had the image of a cartoon character. His mimicry and pantomime kept his teammates in stitches. Teammate Norm Miller once called him an "unconventional liver."

Miller told of an unannounced visit that he and his wife once made to Rader's home in Houston. When Rader saw the Millers'

Rader was nicknamed the Red Rooster for his fiery temperament.

car pull up, he took off his clothes and greeted the couple wearing only a smile.

"Even as well as I knew Doug, I wasn't ready for that," Miller said. "And my wife obviously wasn't.

"I roomed with him for two seasons, but I got tired of him giving me airplane spins over his head. You could never turn your back on him."

Rader believed that being a character was something that you had to work up to; you had to serve an apprenticeship. Rader served his in Northbrook, Illinois, where most of his young friends were "rowdy and hotheaded," as he once described them.

After high school, where he starred in several sports, Rader got a baseball and basketball scholarship to Illinois Wesleyan University. To earn money while at college, he signed a semi-pro hockey contract. He was paid $50 a game to play center and left wing for Peoria in a Midwest industrial league. Since Rader was receiving money, he was no longer an amateur. This could have cost him his scholarship. To prevent the authorities from finding out, he played hockey under the name of Dominic Bulganzio. "I wanted to be the first Italian hockey star," Rader once told *Sport* magazine. Dominic Bulganzio lasted for two years.

In 1964, Doug Rader put his own name on a contract with the Houston Astros. He received a $25,000 bonus for signing.

It was several seasons before Rader began to be noticed. His rookie season with the Astros was 1967. He didn't win a regular spot with the team until 1969. He was awarded the Gold Glove as the league's best defensive third baseman in 1974, and then proceeded to win the award four more years in a row.

He made some incredible plays at third base. In a game at Dodger Stadium, Wes Parker was on second base when Jim LeFebvre drilled a screamer down the line. Parker took off for third, certain the ball would be a base hit. Diving to his right and backward, Rader gloved the ball on one hop while his body was parallel to the ground, bounced to his feet, and was waiting at third to tag Parker when he arrived. Parker called it "the greatest play I have seen in my ten years in baseball."

During his first years with the team, Rader collected bubble gum cards of players only he, nobody else, thought deserved acclaim. Brant Alyea, an outfielder for the Twins, and Houston shortstop Leon McFadden were among those included in his collection. He taped their cards over his locker.

Rader never won any awards as a hitter. While he had good power and got more than his share of timely hits, he was streaky, suffering through long bleak periods. Extra batting practice seldom helped him overcome his slumps. "It's like I'm in quicksand," he once said. "The harder I try, the more I sink."

One year, Rader got off to a very slow start, and for a time was hitting .150, the lowest average among regulars in the National League. "When I see my name at the bottom of the averages, it makes me feel strong," he told a writer. "I have all those names above me to keep up."

As a trickster, Rader was in a class by himself. He once drove a motorcycle into a brick wall on purpose. He once switched the contents of the clubhouse bottles of mouthwash and after-shave lotion. Some players moaned about burning cheeks; others, burning throats.

During a cold early-season game in Montreal, Rader set fire to a number of baseballs by feeding them into the gas heater that was warming the dugout.

Rader's antics were well known in San Diego even before he was traded there in 1975. The season before, Ray Kroc, owner of the Padres, while watching his team lose to Rader's team, took the microphone at San Diego Stadium and said:

"Ladies and gentlemen, I suffer with you. I have never seen such stupid ball playing in my life."

Kroc's words were meant for the Padres. But Rader and his teammates felt they also had been slighted. "Who does he think we are," Rader asked, "a bunch of short-order cooks or something?" (Kroc was the man who had founded the McDonald's hamburger chain.)

Kroc reacted good-naturedly to what Rader said. He announced that he would host a Short-Order Cook Night at San Diego Stadium the next time the Astros came to town. Everyone wearing a chef's hat would be admitted to the ball park free.

On the night the game was played, Rader wore a chef's hat and apron, and he carried the lineup card to home plate in a frying pan, flipping it with a pancake turner.

"Boys," he said to the umpires. "What's your pleasure—rare, medium, or well done?"

Many of Rader's best pranks took place after he had become a member of the Padres. Once, on a flight out of Montreal, Rader took a seat next to Mike Ivie, a young player from Georgia who was known to fear flying.

When the plane was airborne, Rader leaned over and whispered to Ivie, "The airlines don't like to talk about it, but I'm sure you want to know about the Laurentian Condition."

"The what?" said Ivie.

"The Laurentian Condition," said Rader. "It forces the snow in eastern Canada to fall up instead of down over the Laurentian Mountains. The pilots see it coming and they have to turn the plane upside down. It's tough on takeoffs and landings."

Ivie's face whitened. He wiped perspiration from his forehead. Rader would not let up. "Look," he said, pointing. "There's snow over the Laurentians."

More than a few people were surprised when Rader was named manager of the Texas Rangers late in 1982. How could someone who enjoyed offering people exploding cigars or squirting folks with a water pistol disguised as a pack of cigarettes ever be expected to handle a major league baseball team?

26

After he became manager of the Texas Rangers in 1982, Rader was less noted for his bizarre behavior.

Joe Klein, the general manager of the Rangers, had the answer to that question. He had looked carefully at Rader's career. He had spent nine of eleven seasons with the Houston Astros and was the team's captain the last two years. He was traded to San Diego for one year before finishing his career as a player with the Toronto Blue Jays. During his time as a major leaguer, he averaged 15 home runs and 70 RBIs per season. He won five Gold Glove awards as a third baseman. Then Rader coached and worked three years as a minor league manager in Hawaii.

"Anyone who does all that is no fluke," said Joe Klein. "That spells stability to me."

Naturally, Klein had heard about all of the wild things that Rader was said to have done. But he felt that they might be more of an asset than a liability. "We needed someone to get the players' attention," Klein said.

Doug Rader could certainly do that.

The Baltimore Orioles, world champions in 1983, had a resident flake in 35-year-old John Lowenstein. Lowenstein, like many flakes, usually denied he was one. "I just like to keep myself entertained," he once told *Sport* magazine. "Baseball is reality at its harshest. It's a stress existence. You have to introduce a fictional world to survive. But I'm not flaky."

Lowenstein's conduct, however, provided evidence to the contrary.

He first began to be known for his wackiness during the years he spent with the Cleveland Indians in the early 1970s. The club had three different color schemes for its uniforms. The management was strict about having players wear the right combination. Lowenstein would show up at the ball park early, before any of the other players had arrived, find out what color scheme had been ordered for the day, and then don the wrong colors. The other players would follow his lead. When everyone was dressed, Lowenstein would change to the right uniform and then seek out the manager. "Those guys have got the wrong uniform on," he'd say. Then he'd laugh heartily while the manager ranted at his teammates.

Another joke of Lowenstein's was to go up to strangers at airports, look at the nametags on their bags, and say, "Hey, if it

Lowenstein gets congratulated by Baltimore third base coach Cal Ripken following home run at Yankee Stadium.

isn't so-and-so. How's the family?" And he would have a long conversation with the person, who believed he really knew him.

Lowenstein was born in Wolf Point, Montana, and brought up in Southern California. He once knocked in 16 runs in a Little League game. Roberto Clemente was his boyhood idol. After completing high school, he was drafted by the Los Angeles Dodgers, who offered him a $50,000 bonus.

But Lowenstein said no to the Dodger offer because he wanted to go to college. He attended the University of California at Riverside, graduating with a degree in anthropology. The Cleveland Indians drafted him after college. "I signed," he once recalled, "because pro ball seemed like something that would be interesting and few people receive a chance to try it."

Lowenstein lived in Las Vegas, not to be close to the gambling casinos, but to be near the mountains, where he often went backpacking. His wife ran a Las Vegas dance studio.

While with the Indians, Lowenstein formed what he called the "Apathy Fan Club." The Indians played their home games in Cleveland Stadium, which had a seating capacity of just over 74,000. Usually about 70,000 of those seats were empty. Lowenstein said that every vacant seat represented a member of his fan club. He declared that he didn't want to be noticed, just ignored.

After seven seasons with the Indians, Lowenstein was traded to the Texas Rangers, where he spent a year. He once went into a Dallas department store, said he was an executive with a shoe company, and ordered a salesman to rearrange the store's display of footwear. Lowenstein was so convincing in the role that the department store invited him to attend a sales meeting to talk about future store displays.

After the 1978 season, in which he hit .222, the Rangers gave up on Lowenstein. That's when Baltimore landed him. "I always thought he could play," said Earl Weaver, the Oriole manager at the time.

Once with the Orioles, Lowenstein became an exceptional handyman, playing left field, right field, first base, and third base. He also served as a pinch hitter and pinch runner.

Still another role he played was official cake tester. Whenever

Lowenstein acknowledges fans who called him back onto the field after he smacked a grand slam homer at Memorial Stadium.

a cake, birthday or otherwise, appeared in the Oriole clubhouse, the call went out for Lowenstein.

"If it is from a known source, I leave it alone," he once said. "But if it is from an unknown source, you never know what viral infections it might carry." In such cases, Lowenstein would plunge a finger into the cake, and then lick the finger. If the cake tasted good, Lowenstein left it alone.

However, if the cake failed to pass his taste test, Lowenstein grabbed a special Louisville Slugger he kept for such occasions, padded slowly toward the cake as if he were stalking a jungle animal, raised the bat in both hands over his head, and while bellowing like a karate master, brought the bat down with all the power he could muster.

The resulting *splat* not only pulverized the cake but often sent the icing into the four corners of the clubhouse. It cost Lowenstein $5 every time he pulled the stunt. That's how much he tipped the clubhouse man to clean up.

One of Lowenstein's most memorable moments in baseball occurred on June 19, 1980. The Orioles were playing the Oakland A's at Baltimore's Memorial Stadium.

In the seventh inning, with the Orioles trailing, 3–2, Lowenstein was called upon to pinch hit for Lenn Sakata with Mark Corey and Al Bumbry on base. Lowenstein drilled a single into the right field corner, scoring Corey and sending Bumbry to third.

Oakland first baseman Jeff Newman took the outfielder's throw and fired it toward second base in an attempt to nail Lowenstein, who was trying to stretch his single into a double. The ball struck Lowenstein in the back of the neck. He went down as if he had been shot. The ball then caromed into center field. Al Bumbry, representing the go-ahead run, trotted home.

But there were no cheers from the crowd. Instead, a terrible silence fell over the stadium, for out at second base Lowenstein lay in a crumpled heap. The trainer and the team's coaches huddled over him. Lowenstein didn't move a muscle. A stretcher was called for.

As his teammates helped to carry him off the field, Lowenstein remained motionless. His eyes never blinked. Team physician Leonard Wallenstein, walking beside the stretcher, looked very grim. Maybe Lowenstein had a concussion, maybe a broken neck. The fans began applauding as the stretcher-bearers crossed the infield. By the time the procession was nearing the dugout, it was an ovation.

Then, just a couple of strides before entering the dugout, Lowenstein shocked his teammates and the fans by suddenly sitting bolt upright on the stretcher and shaking a pair of clenched fists at the cheering crowd. The stretcher then disappeared into the runway leading to the clubhouse.

The fans blinked in amazement, then broke into wild applause.

Later, Lowenstein admitted the happening wasn't entirely spontaneous. "I had it all planned halfway to the dugout," he said. "You have to acknowledge the crowd for cheering like that.

"It was just one of those valuable moments you can't let slip by."

After X-rays, it was determined that Lowenstein had not suffered serious injury, nothing more than a bad bruise. He accepted the news happily. "The joke would have been on me," he said, "if I had a broken neck."

During 1982 and 1983, Lowenstein was platooned in left field. Nevertheless, in those two years he had 39 homers and 126 RBIs in 633 at bats. "I have no desire to play every day; that's too tiring," Lowenstein once said. But he was grinning when he said it.

Jay Johnstone was his name. "Jay the Flake" was what he was often called.

During a major league career that began late in the 1960s and stretched deep into the 1980s, Johnstone played for eight major league teams. On each, he became the head clown and practical

33

joker. A rundown of all of Johnstone's pranks would require a book much bigger than this one. Dozens are well known. He once showed up at batting practice wearing football shoulder pads. Another time, he lit a firecracker at Joe Garagiola's feet as he interviewed Dick Allen on national television. He once joined an all-girl chorus to sing the national anthem before a game at Dodger Stadium. When it rained, Johnstone sometimes wore an umbrella hat.

During the time he was with the Phillies, Johnstone set off firecrackers in the dugout. He once amused himself—but infuriated some of his teammates—by hitting tennis balls into the dugout during a game. He stood in the runway leading to the clubhouse and whacked the balls off a batting tee.

"Lots of people think I'm crazy, from another world," Johnstone said recently. "But that doesn't bother me. Baseball is a business, but you also have to have fun. It makes it easier to win when you do that. And that's one thing I like to do more than anything—win."

Johnstone played for quite a few winners. He was with Philadelphia when the team won the National League's Eastern Division crown in 1976 and 1977, with the Yankees when they captured the World Series in 1978, and a member of the Dodgers when they were Series winners in 1981.

Johnstone, like more than a few flakes, grew up in Southern California. He quarterbacked his high school football team and led the team in rushing. In basketball, he led in rebounds. In baseball, he was the team's leading hitter.

Some thirty-five colleges offered him scholarships, but he turned down the offers to accept $35,000 in bonus money from the California Angels. He spent five years in the minors before catch-

A Dodger at the time, Johnstone, here pictured with Steve Garvey (left), clowns for photographers wearing Yankee jacket.

ing on with the Angels in 1968 as the team's center fielder.

When Johnstone was with the Yankees in 1978, he once made catcher Thurman Munson the target of a gag. There was a big glass cooler in the Yankee clubhouse for soft drinks. Someone put a watermelon in the cooler to be chilled. Johnstone took the watermelon, drew a face and sideburns on it, put a Yankee hat on it, and placed it back inside the cooler upon a pair of baseball shoes. Johnstone then put Munson's uniform shirt and his catcher's mitt beside the watermelon. The model somehow resembled the original, and the players roared. Munson, however, did not think it was very funny.

From the Yankees, Johnstone was dealt to the Dodgers. There he made his biggest splash.

Tommy Lasorda, the Dodger manager, told Johnstone that the clubhouse was too quiet. "He told me he wanted me to change all that," Johnstone once recalled. He said he wanted me to loosen guys up, make the ball park a fun place to be for them."

Johnstone didn't have to be told twice. One of the first things he did was revive the Green Hornet, a gag that had been started by the Dodgers' Jim LeFebvre and Wes Parker many years before. They would secretly go around spraying a big green GH on players' shoes, their bats, or even the walls of their hotel rooms. Nobody knew the identity of the Green Hornet. The prank drove Lasorda, then a coach, batty. It upset Dodger manager Walter Alston, too.

Johnstone became the "new" Green Hornet in 1981. He got several of his teammates to conspire with him, including pitchers Don Stanhouse and Jerry Reuss, and also first baseman Steve Garvey, who had never been thought of as a cutup.

"Those guys took the heat off me," Johnstone said. Lasorda was a frequent target of Johnstone and his cohorts. "We spray-painted Tommy's shoes and a bottle of wine green. We even spray-painted a big GH on one of his bedsheets.

"We really had Tommy going. He'd come to me and say, 'Jay, I know you're the Green Hornet. But it's impossible to prove because you've been with me all those times.' "

Johnstone pulled off one of his most famous tricks during spring training one year. The Dodgers, as usual, were quartered

As a member of the Cubs in 1983, Johnstone was still clowning.

at Vero Beach, where boredom was normal. Johnstone decided to do something to relieve the monotony.

The team was scheduled to leave on a three-hour bus trip to Orlando to play an exhibition game against the Minnesota Twins. The bus was due to depart at 7:30 A.M. That meant that Lasorda would have to get up around six o'clock in order to have breakfast.

"Tommy has never met a meal he hasn't liked," Johnstone once observed. "He wasn't about to skip breakfast."

The trick was well planned. The night before, Jay got a master key and slipped into Lasorda's room to remove parts from Lasorda's telephone. He knew that Lasorda always left a wake-up call with the operator at the hotel switchboard. But on this night the message would never get through because Johnstone had tampered with the telephone.

Lasorda became furious the next morning when he awakened, glanced at the clock, and found that he had overslept by almost an hour. Unless he hurried, he knew he'd miss breakfast. His mood worsened when he tried to leave his room. The door wouldn't open. Johnstone had tied a rope from the knob, through a window, to a big palm tree.

Lasorda picked up the phone to call the front desk. But because of the missing parts, he couldn't get through.

Then he went berserk. Dodger pitcher Steve Howe, in an adjacent room, remembers hearing Lasorda shout a stream of unprintable words for fully fifiteen minutes. Ted Power, another Dodger pitcher, said he was awakened by Lasorda's screams. And Power was sleeping two rooms away.

A hotel employee finally heard Lasorda and let him out. He managed to get to the team bus before it left but missed breakfast. Upon seeing Johnstone, Lasorda shouted, "Just stay away from me today. Just stay out of my sight."

Once, during a game at Dodger Stadium, Johnstone thought it would be a good idea to drag the infield. This dragging had nothing to do with drag bunting. Johnstone decided to become a temporary member of the Dodger grounds-keeping crew.

Pitcher Jerry Reuss agreed to be Johnstone's accomplice. Just before the home half of the fifth inning began, the two men raced through the stands to the grounds-keepers' quarters, and there changed from their own uniforms into those worn by the grounds crew. They then dragged the infield, hauling the heavy implements used to smooth the ground's surface back and forth between first base and third base.

Meanwhile, teammate Rick Monday had the cameraman for the stadium's scoreboard television follow the pair around the bases. When the fans caught on to what was happening, they began laughing and applauding. When Tommy Lasorda caught on, he immediately fined the pair $200.

When Johnstone and Reuss completed their chores and left the field by the exit on the first base side of Dodger Stadium, they received a standing ovation. They raced back to the grounds-crew's quarters and changed back into their baseball attire.

Johnstone knew he had to change as fast as he could. Burt Hooton, the Dodger pitcher, was having problems on the mound, and Johnstone figured Lasorda would be calling on him to pinch-hit in the bottom of the half of the inning when Hooton was scheduled to hit. Johnstone finished dressing and ran toward the dugout. Just as he got there, he heard Lasorda screaming, "Where's Johnstone? Where's Johnstone? I want Johnstone to hit!"

Johnstone was out of breath. Even so, he grabbed a bat and ran out to the plate. He had no idea that he and Reuss had been fined $200 for their prank.

Johnstone took a pitch and the count went to 2-and-1. On the next pitch, Johnstone slammed a screaming line drive that sailed over the fence in right field for a two-run homer.

As he finished circling the bases and entered the jubilant dugout, Johnstone went over to Lasorda and said, "Next time you need me, just holler." His teammates rolled on the floor in laughter.

Once, in recalling this tale, Johnstone said, "You know, I don't

Another free spirit greets Johnstone in the Chicago outfield.

plan those kinds of things. It's all spontaneous, ad libs. You have to know the situation. You have to pick your spots."

Johnstone clowned around just as much in post-season play as he did during the regular season. He tried on Halloween masks at his locker a half an hour before the Dodgers took the field for a one-game playoff against the Montreal Expos (a game which they won). He also stuffed pillows beneath his jersey and masqueraded as the portly Lasorda. For the World Series that year, in which the Dodgers faced the Yankees, Johnstone donned a Darth Vader mask.

His joking around didn't seem to hurt Johnstone's performance. He lashed a pinch-hit home run that helped bring the Dodgers back in the fourth game, which they eventually won. The team then went on to win the next two games and wrap up the championship.

A hero, Johnstone quickly went from the heights to the depths. Early the next season, he was dropped by the Dodgers.

"Lasorda called me into his office," Johnstone once recalled, "and told me that I was being released. There were tears in his eyes and he hugged me. He told me that it wasn't his decision but that it had been made by the front office. They wanted to go with a younger player."

Johnstone was 36 years old at the time, and in his thirteenth year in the major leagues. He had been used only as a pinch hitter that season and had appeared in thirteen games.

During his career, Johnstone had played for eight different teams. One of those was Philadelphia, where Dallas Green had been the general manager. Green held that position with the Cubs in 1982. He thought that Johnstone could still hit and also be a "loose" influence on the young Cub players. So Chicago signed him up.

The Cubs had finished at the bottom of the National League's Eastern Division in 1980 and 1981, and were seeking to escape last place again when Johnstone joined the team. "I'm trying to help them start to climb," he said.

In the clubhouse, Johnstone was his usual self. When Bill

Buckner made an error on a pop foul, Johnstone brought him a lampshade to replace his glove.

Johnstone, like others of his breed, will be remembered for his ability to blot out the daily tedium that can plague the life of the professional baseball player. That's surely how his teammates will remember him. As one Dodger player put it after learning the club had released Johnstone in 1981, "He was my favorite Martian."

(3)

A Strain on the Head

When pitcher Mark Lemongello joined the Houston Astros in 1976, he was hailed for his enormous potential. But he never lived up to it. After a rookie season in which he won three of four decisions, Lemongello began losing regularly. Most of his losses were accompanied by wild displays of temper. His teammates got so they would hurry to the clubhouse after each defeat just to watch the show.

Lemongello would destroy everything in sight—mirrors, hair dryers, the shelving in his locker. Once he kicked a cigarette machine and the flying glass cut him up. Another time he bit his shoulder so hard it bled.

Lemongello admitted that his temper was a problem. "But," he protested, "I was the only guy on the team that wanted to win. Everyone else was content to lose and it frustrated me pitching in that atmosphere."

Lemongello's rage at losing, however, predated his days with

Mark Lemongello—his temper was a problem.

the Astros. A player who had been a teammate of Lemongello's in the minor leagues remembered him coming into the clubhouse after a tough loss and throwing himself headlong onto the buffet table. "He just lay there covered with mustard and butter for about a half an hour."

Year in, year out, pitchers lead the major leagues in wackiness. Although it would not be fair to say that Mark Lemongello is typical of all pitchers, his is no isolated case, either.

"Pitching," as former umpire Ron Luciano once noted, "must put a strain on the head as well as on the arm. That's the only

44

way," Luciano concluded, "to account for all those pitchers who are certified flakes."

Sportswriter Jim Benagh had another reason. He once noted that since pitchers work many fewer days than their colleagues, usually only one day in every four or five, they have a greater amount of time to create mischief.

Whatever the reason, baseball abounds in loony pitchers. One was relief pitcher Don Stanhouse, who was obtained by the Orioles in 1978. That Stanhouse was a flake was obvious from his nickname—"Stan the Man Unusual" (a parody of Stan "The Man" Musial).

Stanhouse's locker in the Oriole clubhouse also provided evidence of his nuttiness. It bulged with street signs from assorted American League cities, pictures of everyone on the team, a stereo system, two stuffed monkeys, and two stuffed frogs.

Stanhouse could sometimes be seen pouring beer into the mouths of the toy animals after a good game. "If I celebrate," he said, "I want everyone to celebrate."

Stanhouse had little regard for Oriole rules of conduct. At team meetings, he read the newspaper. "He's fabulous," a teammate once said of him. "He does what the rest of us would like to do, but are too chicken to try."

It's usual for pitchers to run sprints in the outfield when they're not scheduled to pitch. Not Stanhouse. "I'm totally against any form of exertion when I don't pitch," he once told *Sport*. "That's the way it has to be.

"When I pitch, I'm a beast. All my energy goes into every pitch. But when I'm off, I'm *off*. I'll do what I want to do. Running? It makes me tired."

Stanhouse became a free agent and joined the Los Angeles

45

Stanhouse tends his "pet" gorilla in the Oriole locker room.

Dodgers in 1980. There, injuries sidelined him for a time and he gave up his flaky behavior, but shortly after his health improved he teamed up with Jerry Reuss to tie manager Tommy Lasorda's shoelaces together while he was being interviewed on network television.

Relief pitcher Al Hrabosky, like Stanhouse, had a nickname that indicated he did not always have both oars in the water. Hrabosky was known as The Mad Hungarian.

Hrabosky's nickname was The Mad Hungarian.

When brought into a game, Hrabosky would put on quite a show. Before throwing a pitch, he would stand behind the pitcher's mound and work himself into a frantic state. His shoulders would twitch, the muscles in his face tighten. And all the while he would be raging at himself. Hrabosky would conclude the performance by taking the ball in his left hand and slamming it as hard as he could into his glove. Then he was ready to pitch.

Why did he do it?

Al Hrabosky, the intimidator

"I did it to stay in the major leagues," explained Hrabosky, who spent a number of years with the Cardinals and then the Royals before turning free agent and signing with the Atlanta Braves in 1980. "I started walking off the mound to concentrate, to psych myself up. I wanted to be intimidating. But I was 5-foot-9, 180 pounds. When I stepped off the mound, I thought of myself as bigger. The Mad Hungarian was 6-foot-4, 280 pounds—and ugly."

On one memorable day, Hrabosky was called into the game in a critical situation. He threw a few warm-up pitches and then went into his routine. Just before he was to deliver his first pitch, he took the ball in his left hand and fired it as hard as he could at his glove.

But he missed the glove. The ball bounded toward second base.

While Hrabosky scampered after the ball, the players in the opposing team's dugout howled in laughter. Hrabosky did not think it was very funny.

Left-hander Bill Lee, who won 119 games and lost 90 during a fourteen-year career with the Red Sox and Expos that ended in 1982, was another free-spirited soul. He once went to the mound wearing a coonskin cap. Another time, it was a gas mask. A Lee trademark was jumping in front of the lens of the nearest TV camera and waving madly whenever a foul ball came within range.

From California, Lee stood 6-foot-2 and weighed 195 pounds. He was always being quoted. Of the light-hitting California Angels, Lee once said: "They could take batting practice in the lobby of the Grand Hotel and not bother a chandelier."

A writer for *Sport* magazine once asked Lee, "What do you think of President Jimmy Carter?"

"He can't hit high fastballs and has trouble with the curve," was Lee's reply.

Another time, Lee was asked, "When you pitch, what do you most often think about?"

"I most often think about not trying to think," Lee declared. "Thinking only gets you in trouble."

Still another time, *Sport* asked Lee, "Why doesn't baseball, in an effort to speed up the game, change its rules and go to a three-ball and three-strike count?"

"Why don't they go to three balls and *two* strikes?" said Lee. "Or just eliminate the pitchers and put the ball on a batting tee? Soon you could have all the managers sit down there in Florida with presto boards and they could conduct the season electronically."

On the mound, Lee would wander about and sometimes field grounders between his legs and behind his back. One year, he developed a pitch he called the moon ball. It traveled in a banana-shaped arc at a very slow speed. Tony Perez hit a home run off it in the sixth inning of the seventh game of the 1975 World Series. The homer got the Reds back into a game they eventually won. Little was heard of the moon ball after that.

Lee spoke out on such topics as racism and industrial pollution, on gun control and birth control. His fans included those who listened to late night radio talk shows and readers of underground newspapers.

Lee's opinions often clashed with those of his employers. One such conflict short-circuited his career. Not long after the season opened in 1982, the Expos released Lee's friend and teammate Rodney Scott. Lee screamed that they couldn't do that to such a nice guy, and stomped out of the ball park in protest.

Lee won 119 games and lost 90 during 14-year major league career.

Lee had once walked out on the Red Sox after they had sold the contract of his friend Bernie Carbo. That protest had lasted twenty-four hours. Lee was then taken back by the team.

Owner John McHale of the Expos was not so forgiving. Lee was fined $5,000 and released. The Expos, however, agreed to pay his salary through the end of the 1982 season.

After his release, Lee telephoned most of the other National League teams about employment. But many didn't even bother to call him back.

Lee, who lived with his wife and children in Longueuil, Quebec, ended by playing baseball for the Senateurs of the Quebec

Senior League that season. He told a visitor that when he was not pitching, playing first base, or the outfield, he spent his time fishing or white-water rafting with his wife and kids. It seemed like an ideal life for a free spirit.

We cannot forget Moe Drabowsky, a pitcher for seven different teams in a career that spanned almost two decades. Midway in that career, Drabowsky was traded from Kansas City to Baltimore. On a subsequent road trip that took the Orioles to Kansas City, Drabowsky remembered you could call the home bullpen from the visitor's bullpen phone. At the first opportunity, he telephoned the Kansas City bullpen, imitated the voice of manager Al Dark, and declared, "Get Krausse throwing." Imagine Dark's bewilderment when he looked out at the bullpen and saw Lew Krausse warming up.

That wasn't the end of it. The next day, Drabowsky rang up the bullpen again, imitated the voice of Kansas City owner Charlie Finley, and demanded an explanation of the entire matter.

On more than one occasion, Drabowsky made long-distance calls from bullpen phones. Once he even called Europe.

It was Drabowsky who, during the 1969 World Series, hired a plane to fly over the Baltimore ball park towing a sign that read: BEWARE OF MOE.

There's nothing new about pitchers' nutty conduct. It can be traced to every baseball era. During the 1920s, the Brooklyn Dodgers had a pitcher named Clyde (Pea Ridge) Day who would stand on the mound after he had struck out the last man in an inning and let loose an ear-splitting hog call. The Dodgers of that time were managed by Wilbert Robinson, known affectionately as Uncle Robbie. Pea Ridge's antics were even too much for the easy-going Uncle Robbie, and he ordered him to put an end to the hog calling. "A man," Uncle Robbie said, "has no right to be sillier than God made him."

Pea Ridge had many other talents. He was very proud of his ability to expand his chest. He would borrow a belt from one of his Dodger teammates, buckle it around his chest, and then expand his chest and snap the belt. The trick was always good for a laugh.

Some of his teammates once ordered a special belt from a harness-maker. It looked like an ordinary belt but it was tremendously strong. The belt was given to Pea Ridge, who fastened it around his chest, took a deep breath, expanded, and then waited for something to happen. His eyes bulged. The veins in his neck stood out. His face reddened. Then suddenly Pea Ridge screamed in pain and grabbed his side. Pea Ridge had cracked two ribs.

Two other old-time pitchers, Al Schacht and Max Patkin, must be mentioned here. They managed to turn their talents for zaniness into full-time careers. Schacht, who pitched for the Washington Senators in the 1920s, won much greater fame entertaining crowds at minor league and major league ball parks. His marvelous mimicry and pantomime earned him the title of the "Clown Prince of Baseball."

Max Patkin was also successful as a baseball clown. Patkin worked mostly at minor league parks. Unlike Schacht, he never pitched in the major leagues, only the minors.

In recent times, clowns such as Patkin and Schacht have been supplanted by such individuals as Ted Giannoulas. Giannoulas entertains fans as The Chicken (formerly the San Diego Chicken). There is also the Philly Phan-atic, the Baltimore Oriole, and so on. It is a long list. Pitchers who are exceptional flakes can't depend on their wackiness for employment anymore.

The subject is noses, as Max Patkin (left) clowns with Billy Martin.

Pitchers are sometimes accused of strange conduct concerning the baseballs they throw. They doctor them. A dab of moisture, such as saliva or sweat, creates resistance as the ball travels through the air, causing it to do unexpected things.

Cutting the ball, even putting a small nick in it, accomplishes the same thing. Rick Honeycutt, while pitching for Seattle in 1980, was found to be wearing a flesh-colored Band-Aid with a thumbtack sticking out of it. No one proved that Honeycutt was using the thumbtack to scratch up baseballs, but the offense earned him a ten-day suspension, nevertheless.

A doctored pitch is a hard pitch to control. It could easily hit the batter, baseball officials claim. That's why such pitches have been made illegal.

Of course, a pitcher doesn't use a doctored pitch as his main pitch. It's a "situation" pitch, used to get him out of tight spots. It used to be said of Whitey Ford, the Yankee lefty, that he was so slick in doctoring the ball he could carve his initials in it and not get caught. Whitey loved to throw a dirty ball. He dirtied it on one side only. That meant that when the ball was on its way to the plate, rotating as it traveled, it created an optical illusion. All the batter saw was half of it.

Whitey had an exceptional curve and near-perfect control. The dirty ball made him that much tougher.

Bill Kinnamon, an American League umpire during the 1960s, once recalled throwing out a new ball to Ford. Before Ford's first pitch, Yogi Berra went to the mound to talk to him. Yankee infielders Bobby Richardson and Tony Kubek joined the conference. All the time they spoke, they were rubbing the ball. Finally, the three men went back to their positions and Ford got set to pitch.

The batter, Charlie Maxwell of the White Sox, stepped out of the batter's box, and asked Kinnamon to look at the ball.

Kinnamon frowned. "I just threw him a new one," he said.

"I know this guy better than you do," Maxwell replied. "Check it."

When Kinnamon looked at the ball, he couldn't believe what he saw. Ford had gotten it so dirty it couldn't possibly be used. "I had to throw it out and give him a new one," Kinnamon said. "He just stood there, grinning and rubbing it up again."

Sometimes Ford would get help from his catcher. The Yankees never wanted an umpire to throw a new ball directly to Ford.

Ford was said to be superslick when it came to doctoring the ball.

The umpire was supposed to give the ball to the catcher first.

"Now when you handed the ball to Elston Howard," Kinnamon once recalled, "he all of a sudden had the worst hands in the world. You could *lay* it in his hands, and he couldn't hold it."

When Howard went to pick up the ball, he'd rub it along the ground, loading up the seams with dirt. Then Howard would trot out to the mound and hand the ball to Whitey. "Ford would put enough slime on it to get half the ball dirty by the time Ellie got back to the plate," Kinnamon said.

The spitball is the most frequently used of all the illegal pitches. To throw a spitter, the pitcher moistens the first two or three fingers of his hand, keeping the thumb dry. For moisture, it doesn't actually have to be saliva; any slippery substance can serve the purpose.

The ball is thrown like a fastball, but the moisture allows it to be released with no spin. As the ball nears the plate, it drops suddenly. When thrown sidearm, it veers to either the right or left.

When it came to wetting up the ball, the most skilled practitioner in recent years was Gaylord Perry. Perry had enormous success once he had hitters convinced he was throwing wet stuff. He became the first pitcher in forty-eight years to win 20 games in both leagues when he soared to a 24–6 record with the Cleveland Indians in the American League in 1972. He had won 23 games for San Francisco in the National in 1970.

Perry was the only pitcher to win the Cy Young Award in both leagues—in 1972 with Cleveland, in 1978 with San Diego.

In 1983, wearing the uniform of the Seattle Mariners, Perry won his 300th game. His lifetime record was 311–247. Perry made spit pay better than any other pitcher before or since.

In his autobiography, *Me and the Spitter*, Perry confessed. He said he threw a spitball "for the first, but hardly the last time" in 1964.

Perry's team, the Giants, was playing the Mets at Shea Stadium. Chris Cannizzaro was the batter. The ball "dipped into the dirt," Perry said, "like a shot quail." Perry threw four more spit-

Perry was to the spitball what Hank Aaron was to the home run.

balls to Cannizzaro, causing Casey Stengel, the New York manager, to shout, "Spitter! Spitter!" from the dugout. Perry finally walked Cannizzaro on a high fastball.

Those first spitballs led Perry through the mudball, the emeryball, the K-Y ball (for K-Y Lubricating Jelly), the vaseline ball, and the sweatball, just to name a few. "During the next eight years or so," he said, "I reckon I tried everything on the old apple but salt and pepper and chocolate sauce toppin'."

Perry said he learned the technique of throwing the spitball from Bob Shaw of the Giants, who had been an 18-game winner for the White Sox. Said Perry: "I had to learn how to load it up, how big a load the ball would carry, where to drop the load, how to grip the ball, and how to release it as well as how to control it. And probably most important of all, how to hide it from four umpires, three coaches, a manager, and twenty-five players on the field as well as spying executives in box seats."

Perry's confession probably would have earned him a heavy fine had he not claimed he was no longer using the spitter, that he had reformed. He said that he had become so skilled in the delivery of the standard pitches—fastballs, curves, and sliders—that he didn't need to wet the ball anymore.

Few major league players believed that Perry's claim was sincere. Up until the very end of his career, Perry was cursed by hitters, inspected by umpires, and screamed at by managers.

Jim Merritt of the Texas Rangers once admitted that he threw spitballs in defeating the Cleveland Indians, 3–0. He described the spitballs he threw as "Gaylord fastballs," and said he threw 25 or 30 of them in the game. Following his statement, Merritt was fined. Ironically, the pitcher Merritt beat was Gaylord Perry.

Of all the pitchers noted for throwing wet baseballs in recent

Jim Merritt called his spitballs "Gaylord fastballs."

years, Perry was the most famous. But Lou Burdette, who won 207 games with several different teams, during the 1950s and 1960s, was a close runner-up. Arthur Daley of the New York *Times* once said that a newspaper needed three columns for Burdette's pitching record: won, lost, and relative humidity.

(4)

Rare Bird

If awards were handed out for zany conduct in baseball, the biggest, shiniest trophy in recent years would have gone to a gangly, curly-haired, right-handed pitcher named Mark Fidrych, a rookie with the Detroit Tigers in 1976. Fidrych had a 19–9 record that season, led the American League with a 2.34 earned run average, and was named Rookie of the Year in the American League.

But his exceptional skills were not what made Fidrych (pronounced FID-rich) the biggest sensation in baseball in decades. Simply stated, Mark Fidrych made baseball fun.

People noticed Fidrych at first because he talked to the baseball when he was pitching. He'd hold it in front of his face, almost as if it were an ice cream cone he was about to munch, and give it whatever commands suited the situation. If the ball happened to be riding high, he'd say, "Get down! Get down!

"Come on now, curve," he'd order. "We gotta curve!"

When he talked to the ball, he was really reminding himself

what to do, Fidrych once explained. "It's just my way of keeping my head together and keeping my concentration," he said.

Fidrych also stomped around on the mound and talked to himself. "Get it over . . . Come on now, get it over . . . I gotta throw hard . . . Let it flow . . . Let it flow . . . Slow the body and let it fly."

He had other wacky habits. After the third out of an inning, Fidrych would race back to the dugout, whereas most pitchers walk. But Fidrych wanted to be sure to be there when his infielders and outfielders arrived so he could thank them for what they had done during the inning.

Fidrych had another unusual ritual he would employ whenever a batter touched him for a base hit. When the ball was returned to him, Fidrych would walk off the mound and lob the ball to the umpire and ask for a new one.

"It's in my mind that the ball has a hit in it," he explained.

Unless the ball was badly marred, the umpire would stuff it into his jacket pocket along with the others. It undoubtedly reappeared later in the game. But that didn't bother Fidrych. "At least I don't *know* it's the same ball," he said.

Everyone agreed that Mark was not simply clowning around. He did not plan his antics in advance. He was being completely natural in what he did. Talking to the ball, talking to himself, and running to and from the dugout—these were as much a part of his normal pitching routine as taking signs from the catcher and covering first base on bunts.

Because of the way he flapped about on the mound, Fidrych was nicknamed The Bird. Then people began saying that he resembled Big Bird, one of the stars of "Sesame Street." Everytime he pitched, the fans chanted, "Go, Bird, go! Go, Bird, go!" And they danced in the aisles in bird costumes.

Fidrych was American League Rookie of the Year in 1976.

Fidrych, The Bird, poses with Sesame Street's Big Bird.

Fidrych turned Detroit upside down. Fans by the thousands purchased "Bird" T-shirts and orange-and-black buttons blazoned with the phrase "The Bird Is the Word." Youngsters strode through the stands carrying signs hailing their hero. MARK, WE LOVE YOU, one read.

A couple announced they were naming their newborn son for

Mark. A radio station listener called in to propose that Fidrych be named the official state bird of Michigan, replacing the robin. A Michigan state legislator introduced a resolution requesting that the Tigers boost Fidrych's salary, which, at the time, was the major league minimum for rookies.

Detroit and, eventually the entire nation had a love affair with young Mark Fidrych. It's a shame it didn't last longer.

Mark Fidrych was born on August 14, 1954, in Worcester, in central Massachusetts. He grew up in nearby Northboro, population 9,218.

He had one older sister and two younger ones. He was very close to his mother, who called him Markie.

Mark's dad, a high school teacher and later a principal, was a good athlete who especially enjoyed bowling. His father got Mark interested in sports when he was very young. Mark's first appearance on television was on a bowling show when he was a little boy.

By the time he was four or five, Mark was already interested in baseball. His mother used to tell interviewers that he wouldn't let her tuck him into bed at night until he had put his glove under his mattress. After a kiss good-night, Mark would pull the peak of his cap over his eyes and go to sleep.

Besides sports, Mark, as a teenager, liked cars. He worked part-time at a local gas station. His ambition was to own a '57 Chevy and hop it up. Even during his teens, his mother once said, he continued to enjoy "Sesame Street," although he never saw any connection between himself and Big Bird.

Mark played Little League baseball and later pitched for Algonquin High School. He first began to attract attention in the summer of 1971 as a pitcher for a local American Legion team. He was sixteen, tall and lean, with a shaggy mop of hair.

He threw hard, low strikes, and had excellent control. When a teammate made a good play, Mark would rush up to him and let him know. He talked to the ball, too. But nobody thought anything about it. "He was a free spirit," his manager, Ted Rolfe, once said of him. "He did what he wanted, but he never caused any trouble." In three years in American Legion baseball, Mark won 16 and lost only 3.

Crowds of 1,500 to 1,700 would turn out to watch Mark. The more important the game, the tighter the situation, the better Mark pitched.

Major league scouts began showing up for Mark's games. Joe Cusick, the scout for the Tigers in New England, was more interested in Mark than any of the others. He recommended that the Tigers draft Mark, and the club followed his recommendation, selecting him in the tenth round of the 1974 draft. It was not a move that made headlines. Well over two hundred players were drafted before Mark.

The Tigers offered Mark a bonus of $10,000. At the time, Mark was working in a Northboro gas station for $2 an hour. "I couldn't believe it," he said. "I would have signed for free."

After he signed, Detroit sent Mark to Bristol (Virginia) in the Appalachian League. You could go no lower in the Detroit farm system.

The first time he set foot on the field, Mark startled his teammates with the high-pitched squawk that would later become one of his trademarks. "*Gaawk! Gaawk! Gaawk!*" shrilled Fidrych as he loped about the field.

"A bird! You're a bird!" declared Bristol coach Jeff Hogan.

That's how his nickname came to be.

"He talked like the devil to the ball and everyone else," Joe Lewis, the Bristol manager, once recalled. "He was just intense. And he really worked hard, really pitched for me. "He was so reliable I started using him all the time. One bit of trouble and I'd send him in and he'd get them out."

The next year, Mark moved up the ladder to Lakeland (Florida) in the Florida State League. Next, it was Montgomery (Alabama) in the Southern League. He spent only fifteen days there before being promoted to the Tigers' top farm club at Evansville (Indiana) in the American Association. Pitching against the best minor league hitters in the country, Mark quickly racked up a 4-and-1 record, with a 1.59 earned run average.

The Tiger organization was seriously interested in Mark by this time. Word of his talents had not only reached Detroit, but tales of his antics had, too.

When he won the game that clinched the divisional title for the final out, he gave the center fielder a big hug and kiss.

That fall Mark pitched at Dunedin in the Florida Instructional League, where he made a stunning impression on the Tiger brass. By the time league competition had ended, Tiger manager Ralph Houk felt certain that Mark was going to be a major league pitcher.

Mark didn't pitch particularly well at training camp the next spring. But that didn't matter. It had already been decided that he would be Detroit's fifth starting pitcher once the season began.

Bad weather caused a bunch of postponements early in the season, so the veteran starters got all the pitching assignments. Mark was passed over time after time.

Instead of pitching, he threw along the sidelines and shagged fly balls in the outfield to keep in shape. Or he would sprint across the outfield from one foul line to the other with the other pitchers. Fidrych always ran faster and farther than anyone.

He cheered on his teammates during games with a stream of shrieking chatter that never stopped.

Mark pitched briefly in two games. Manager Ralph Houk brought him in from the bullpen in the ninth inning of a game against the Oakland A's in mid-April. It was not a promising debut. He made two pitches, one of which Oakland's Don Baylor slammed into left field for a single that won the game.

Fidrych did not let himself get upset by that turn of events. Quite the opposite. When the teams were taking batting practice the next night, Fidrych went up to Baylor and said to him, "Everyone gets a lucky hit once in a while."

Baylor, a veteran who was much respected by his teamates and rival players, could hardly believe his ears.

"I told him," said Baylor, "he ought to wait until he's been around here for a while before he starts talking like that."

Fidrych pitched an inning of relief against the Minnesota Twins early in May. Nothing that he did in that game gave the slightest indication of what was to come.

Fidrych finally got his first starting assignment on a Saturday afternoon in mid-May that year. The Cleveland Indians furnished the opposition. Less than 15,000 fans were in the stands at Tiger Stadium.

The day was dreary and overcast. A persistent drizzle began falling early in the afternoon, causing the game to be delayed for almost half an hour.

The umpires finally ordered the tarp removed from the infield. Fidrych went out to the mound.

Fidrych liked to manicure the mound before each inning.

The Tigers hoped that Fidrych would last for five or six innings, and then a relief pitcher would take over. No one was prepared for what he did. He retired the first fourteen batters to face him, held the Indians hitless until the sixth inning, went the distance, gave up only two hits, and won, 2–1.

Time after time, he stirred up the fans with his crazy antics. He talked to the ball. He pointed and aimed it at the plate before he threw. And he talked to himself constantly.

He painstakingly manicured the pitching mound before each inning, stooping over and smoothing out the damp soil with his left hand. In the sixth inning, when the grounds keepers wanted to make some minor repairs on the field, Fidrych waved them

69

away from the mound. Instead, he took a handful of sand from their wheelbarrow, and carried it to the mound where he carefully deposited it and then patted it down.

"When I'm pitching, the mound belongs to me," he told reporters after the game.

"I've never seen anything like it," said the Indians' Rico Carty. "Sometimes I was almost laughing. But how can you hit when you're laughing?

"The first time I got up, he pointed the ball at me, and I said to myself, 'What the hell is he doing and saying?' It was like he was trying to hypnotize me.

"I just said, 'Throw the ball.'

"Then he did—and I couldn't hit it."

Buddy Bell, another Cleveland player, said, "He really messes up your concentration. He's always talking to himself—even up until he's getting ready to throw. All you could hear was, 'Okay, ball, we're going to do this or we're going to do that.'"

Right fielder John Lowenstein thought he had a way to cope with Fidrych's strange behavior. He said the next time he faced him he was going to call time and ask the umpire to inspect the ball. Then he said he planned to grab the ball, hold it to his ear, and listen to what Fidrych had told it.

In the weeks that followed, the Fidrych legend built steadily. His next starting assignment was at Boston's Fenway Park, about an hour's drive from Fidrych's home in Northboro. His mother and father and two busloads of Northboro fans were in the stands to cheer him. Mark gave up a home run to Carl Yastrzemski in the fourth inning that boosted Boston into a 2–0 lead. He buckled down after that, but his Tiger teammates were unable to produce any runs, and the score stayed at 2–0.

Talking to the ball became one of Fidrych's trademarks.

In his next starting assignment, against Milwaukee, the Tigers won, 5–4. Early in June, Fidrych beat Bert Blyleven and the Texas Rangers at Arlington Stadium. Back in Detroit, he defeated Nolan Ryan and the California Angels for his fourth victory of the season, his third in a row. He beat Kansas City and Minnesota.

Late in June, against the Red Sox, Fidrych was on his way to his seventh victory, working with a 6–3 lead. There were two out and one on base for Boston in the ninth inning. Then third baseman Aurelio Rodriguez dropped an easy pop fly that should have ended the game.

Many young pitchers would have come apart at that point. Rico Petrocelli, a dangerous hitter came to the plate.

Fidrych, however, seemed more concerned about Rodriguez than himself. He dashed over to third base where he patted the dejected Rodriguez on the back. "Don't worry," he told him. "I'll get Petrocelli."

Then Fidrych went back to the mound and struck out Petrocelli on three pitches.

Afterward, Ralph Houk hailed Mark for what he had done. "You might have thought the kid would go to pieces, but he struck him out," said Houk. "He's got great concentration. That's the biggest thing I've ever seen him do."

Not long after his victory over the Red Sox, Fidrych was named to the American League's All-Star team. He was also beginning to attract attention outside the world of baseball. Feature stories about him appeared in *People, Newsweek,* and *The Wall Street Journal.*

He charmed interviewers with his naturalness and honesty. While other players talked about stocks and bonds, Mark spoke of going home in the winter to pump gas at a Northboro service station. While other players drove flashy and expensive sports cars, Fidrych pulled up to Tiger Stadium in a much-dented Dodge Colt. While other players might dress in vested suits, Mark's favorite uniform consisted of a T-shirt and blue jeans. He complained that the Tigers made him wear "good clothes" when the team traveled.

Sport was one of more than a dozen magazines that had a cover photo of Fidrych.

Fan letters for Fidrych began to pour in daily. Gifts, too. Hundreds of people sent The Bird toy birds.

Lines began forming at Tiger Stadium for a Monday night game against the New York Yankees. One of the best hitting teams in baseball at the time, the Yankees held an 11-game lead over the Tigers, who had lost more games than they had won, despite Fidrych's heroics. But the game loomed as a sellout because Fidrych was scheduled to pitch.

Network television cameras added to the excitement. ABC-TV was telecasting the contest as part of its summer-long "Game-of-the-Week" package. Tens of millions of Americans were to be introduced to the bird phenomenon.

When The Bird went to the mound for the first time and got down on his knees and began to make things shipshape, the crowd stood and cheered. The Yankee players gaped open-mouthed.

Outfielder Mickey Rivers, who boasted a 20-game hitting streak, was the first Yankee batter. Fidrych wiggled his knees and shook his wrist before pitching to Rivers, who grounded out. After another out, Fidrych ended the inning by striking out Chris Chambliss, the New York first baseman. The final pitch broke so sharply that Chambliss never bothered to take the bat off his shoulder.

The Tigers produced two runs in the bottom half of the first inning on a home run by Rusty Staub. The Yanks came back with a run in the second when Elrod Hendricks slammed a homer into the right field stands. But after that, Fidrych settled down and shut out the Yankees the rest of the way.

He talked to the ball and chatted with himself throughout the game. He seemed not to notice that the crowd spent about half of the night chanting, "Go, Bird, go! Go, Bird, go!"

Fidrych's teammates supported him with three more runs, which gave him a 5–1 victory. When the final out was registered, The Bird flew off the mound as if he had just won the seventh game of the World Series. He hugged teammates, coaches, grounds keepers, security guards—anyone. He waved his hat and pranced around.

Bob Uecker, a member of the ABC-TV crew at the time, interviewed Fidrych in the dugout after the game. During the interview, fans continued to cheer him. And after he had left the dugout for the clubhouse, thousands remained to chant, "We want The Bird. We want The Bird."

In those days, baseball players never took curtain calls. But Fidrych could hear the chanting and decided that it had to be acknowledged. So he went back out onto the field. But he didn't go alone. He brought Rusty Staub and several other players with him.

Fidrych became the hottest attraction in baseball and a national celebrity that night.

When players for the American and National Leagues assembled in Philadelphia that summer for the All-Star game, Fidrych was the center of attention. That may have been his undoing. Writers, broadcasters, photographers, agents, promoters, and fans beseiged him from the moment he arrived. He did not have a moment's peace.

Just before the game began, President Jerry Ford entered the American League clubhouse. He spotted Fidrych right away.

"You're The Bird!" the President said, sounding excited. "How are you?"

Mark looked up and said, "Did you send me a thing in Texas?" Fidrych asked, meaning a telegram.

"I tried to call you," the President said.

"Yeah, yeah, where's your son? I'd like to talk to him."

"He's around," said the President, referring to his son, Jack.

"Now don't talk to the young fellow, talk to the old man."

"Oh, OK, I was just wondering how he was doing with all those dates."

"You come to Washington," the President said, laughing. "He'll fix you up."

"I may do that," said Fidrych.

Chatting with the President of the United States was the last in a long series of distractions for Fidrych that day. The distractions may have been the reason he pitched one of his worst games of the year, giving up two runs in the first inning, and ending up as the losing pitcher in the American League's 7–1 defeat.

But a few nights later, when the team returned to Detroit, Fidrych got back on the track, shutting out the Oakland A's, 1–0, in eleven innings.

All in all, it was an extraordinary season for Fidrych. He finished with a 19–9 record. His nineteen wins were the most by a Tiger rookie in sixty-eight years. His earned run average of 2.34 was the lowest in the major leagues for a starting pitcher. He was only the second rookie to start the All-Star game. He was named Rookie of the Year in the American League and major league Man of the Year by the National Association of Professional Baseball Leagues.

But more important, the 21-year-old Fidrych had completely captivated the world of baseball with his antics. "I've never seen anything like this in my life," Dick Tracewski, a Tiger coach, told newspaperman Jim Benagh during the season. "I played with Denny McLain [the former Tiger who won 31 games in 1968] and I roomed with Sandy Koufax [the youngest pitcher ever elected to the Hall of Fame] for three years when he was striking out everybody and winning all those games.

"But nothing like this has ever happened."

The Bird loved all that happened. "You can't explain what's going on," he said during his rookie year. "But I can go out and do things I couldn't do before, maybe go on a vacation for a week and a half, two weeks, and not worry about it. But it can end just like that, too."

It did end "just like that." The downhill slide began the next year during spring training at Lakeland, Florida. The Bird was shagging flies in the outfield, clowning around more than usual. A long, high drive sailed his way. The Bird, whooping and hollering, galloped after it. Eager to make a showboat catch, he leaped higher in the air than was necessary, gloved the ball, then came down on his left foot. He heard a sickening crack and felt a stab of pain in his left knee.

Surgery to repair a damaged cartilage followed. On his return, The Bird won six games in a row, but then he began to have shoulder problems. Doctors said it was tendinitis. The Bird ended the season with a 6–4 record.

One bad year followed another. He was 2–0 in 1978, 0–3 in 1979, and 2–3 in 1980. The next year, the Tigers assigned him to their farm team at Evansville (Indiana) in the American Association. He won 6, he lost 3. The Tigers released him.

By this time, Ralph Houk, who had been Fidrych's Tiger manager, had become manager of the Boston Red Sox. Houk brought The Bird to spring training in 1982 before sending him to Pawtucket (Rhode Island), a Red Sox farm club in the International League.

Fidrych's greatest moment that season came in a game he pitched against Dave Righetti of Columbus, who was to go on to stardom with the New York Yankees. Fidrych went nine innings and struck out Butch Hobson, the final batter, to wrap up a 7–5 victory before 9,300 hysterical fans, the biggest crowd in the history of Pawtucket's McCoy Stadium. After the game-ending strikeout, the crowd stood and yelled, "Bird, Bird, Bird," for ten minutes.

But there were more bad days than good that season. Fidrych finished with a 6–8 record.

The saga ended the next year, 1983. After 12 games with

Fidrych ended pitching career with Pawtucket Red Sox in 1983.

Pawtucket, The Bird had a 2–5 record and a 9.68 earned run average. He had given up nearly two hits and a walk for every inning he had pitched. He knew the end was near.

He got the word from Pawtucket manager Tony Torchia in the hotel lobby in West Virginia where the team was playing. Another pitcher was coming off the disabled list. Somebody had to be dropped from the roster to make room for him. Fidrych figured he was the one.

"Well, Mark," manager Torchia said, "things haven't been

working out the way we planned, so we've got to make a decision."
Fidrych interrupted. "I'll make the decision for you," he said.
"I'll just retire."

After his retirement, Fidrych went back home to Blue Water
Ranch, his scruffy 100-acre farm in Northboro. There he tended
his pigs, cows, and geese. "From bullpen to pigpen," said one
newspaper account of what had happened.

Fidrych said he didn't feel shortchanged because arm problems put an end to his career. "I had ten great years of baseball,
no matter if it was the minor leagues or the major leagues," he
said. "I got ten years out of my life where I got to do what I
wanted to do, play baseball.

"I don't think I got cheated. All I have to do is look back at
my friends that I played ball with, and who never even saw a
major league uniform.

"The only time I get depressed is when I pick up the paper
and read how the starting pitchers are flubbing up, and I think,
'Jeez, I could do that.' "

Baseball was much the poorer without The Bird. Pitchers who
talk to baseballs and smooth out the pitcher's mound with their
hands before sellout crowds of screaming, adoring fans don't
come along often enough. Once every century or so is about the
average.

(5)

Dirty Tricks

You've seen this happen many times. A player on the field gets injured during a game and a trainer carrying a medical bag runs out. The grim-faced players stand around while the trainer sizes up the injury. This little drama was unfolding in St. Louis one time, when all of a sudden the players and coaches broke into laughter. When the trainer reached in his bag, there were only a couple of baloney sandwiches there, courtesy of a clubhouse practical joker.

Baseball's flakes thrive on such humor. To some, casting a teammate in an embarrassing situation provides as big a kick as a double with the bases loaded.

Putting knots in a teammate's clothing or nailing a player's shoes to the clubhouse floor are standard practical jokes. But today's wackos have advanced beyond stunts like these, finding them dull and unimaginative. Practical joking has become quite creative.

Take, for instance, the stunt pulled by pitcher Jim Rooker of the Pirates. It is still talked about. One day Rooker arrived early at the ball park, removed all the bottles and shelving from the soft drink cooler in the clubhouse and climbed inside. He waited and waited. Finally, his moment came. John Milner, in quest of a soda, opened the cooler door and reached in. Rooker was ready. He grabbed Milner's hand in his own icy paws and at the same time let out a blood-chilling howl. Long after the incident, Milner remained sitting in one corner of the trainer's room, still visibly shaken.

One mainstay of the practical joker is the hotfoot. The usual hotfoot is executed by sticking a match between the sole and upper of the victim's shoe without his knowing it. Then the match is lit.

The victim may not feel anything right away, which gives the perpetrator the opportunity to steal away. Soon the victim's foot begins to smart, and then the pain becomes serious. The victim leaps up, stamping his foot and screaming. Everyone else roars with laughter.

This technique is for beginners. Baseball's wackos have made tremendous advances in hotfoot technology.

Texas Ranger pitcher Jim Kern employed the explosion technique. Teammate Andy Thornton was one of Kern's early victims. Thornton was asleep in a plane when Kern launched his attack. "I dipped cotton balls in alcohol and rubbed them over his shoes," Kern said in recalling the incident. "When I put a match to them, they went up like a forest fire."

St. Louis Cardinal relief pitcher Mark Littell devised one of the wickedest of all hotfoots. He first spread bubblegum on the victim's shoelaces. "You have to get the gum to the right consistency in your mouth," Littell explained. "It has to be gooey or it won't flame right. Then you put rubbing alcohol on the guy's shoelaces and stick a match in.

"When he reaches down, the gum feels like hot tar. He can't get it off his fingers. It's great, a real panic!"

During the early to mid-1970s, the Yankees had several players who were dedicated practical jokers—Fritz Peterson, Mike Kekich, Steve Kline, Mel Stottlemyre, and Sparky Lyle. They were always pulling stunts, the hotfoot being only one of them.

Peterson often used the names of other Yankee players in filling out order forms for various kinds of merchandise. He would, for example, order sets of encyclopedias in Mel Stottlemyre's name. When Stottlemyre returned home from a road trip, he would often find boxes and boxes of books there, worth many hundreds of dollars, all ordered by Peterson. Stottlemyre would send the encyclopedias back to the publishers. But more kept arriving.

Once, when the Yankees were in Minneapolis to play the Twins, Mike Kekich bought a water bed. He kept bragging about how terrific it was. That was his first mistake. His second was storing the box containing the bed in the clubhouse. When Kekich arrived at the park for a game one day, he was shocked to see his water bed hanging from the flagpole in front of the County Stadium scoreboard. His teammates had struck.

Another time, pitcher Steve Kline received a potted flowering plant from a girlfriend. Steve had never gotten flowers from a woman before, and he thought it was nice. But Steve didn't get much time to enjoy the gift. When he went out onto the field for pregame practice, Peterson poured the contents of a bottle of rubbing alcohol into the flowerpot. The plant was withered and all but dead by the time Kline returned to the clubhouse. Sparky Lyle used to get a kick out of sitting bare-bottomed on cakes. He did it all the time. It started out when Lyle was playing for the Boston Red Sox. One day it was Ken Harrelson's birthday and someone gave him a lemon meringue pie. Harrelson, in a playful mood, shoved the pie in Lyle's face. "I'm going to get even with you for this," Lyle said with a grin, as he wiped the sticky meringue and lemon custard from his face.

A day or two later, someone sent Harrelson a huge birthday cake that had green icing and was shaped like Fenway Park. Harrelson loved it. When Lyle saw the cake, a plot hatched in his mind.

The Red Sox were on the field for batting practice. Lyle left early, went into the clubhouse, took off his clothes, and waited for Harrelson. When he saw Harrelson enter, Sparky yelled out, "Kenny!" to get his attention, and then he plopped down right on top of the cake.

From then on, whenever someone had a birthday and received a cake, the players would yell for Sparky. He'd take off his clothes and sit on it. It was great fun.

When Lyle was traded to the Yankees, he found that his reputation as a cake-sitter had preceded him to New York. He had been with the team only a short time when one of the players announced, "Hey, Sparky, a cake." Sparky did what everyone expected him to do—sat on it.

But his act didn't get the usual response. Instead of laughter, there were gasps. "I can't believe you'd do that," said one player. "Boy, that takes guts," said another. Sparky was puzzled. Then someone told him he had sat on a cake that was intended for Yankee manager Ralph Houk. Sparky shuddered. He had visions

Sparky Lyle—he loved birthdays.

of being shipped out to some minor league club by morning. But
Houk, after growling a bit, went along with the gag.

Sparky sat on more and more cakes. It became standard pro-
cedure in the Yankee clubhouse. Jim Turner, the team's pitching
coach, loved cake. As soon as one arrived in the clubhouse and
the players started yelling for Lyle, Turner would run and get a
knife and try to cut a piece before Sparky flattened it. But Turner
wasn't fast enough. "He never beat me to a cake," Sparky once
boasted. "Not once."

Lyle continued his cake-sitting for several seasons. Then a Los

Angeles newspaper carried a full-page story about the prank. That ended it. Sparky figured the gag was now too well known, and that it would be only a matter of time until someone baked a needle or some other such object into a Yankee cake. Sparky had no wish to see his gag backfire.

Lyle, however, continued in his role as the Yankees' chief practical joker. He once made Yogi Berra the target of one of his pranks. Berra, one of baseball's all-time greats, was a Yankee coach at the time. He became the team's manager in 1984.

"Yogi's supposed to have said a lot of funny things," Lyle said in *The Bronx Zoo,* his book about the Yankees, "but I don't know how anyone hears all those things he says because he doesn't talk."

Besides finding Berra to be silent most of the time, Lyle also discovered him to be very thrifty. One way that Berra cut expenses was by using Lyle's toothpaste. "He'd walk over to my locker and take it," said Lyle. "I guess he wasn't about to buy any."

Lyle decided to try to put an end to the practice. He took a tube of White Heat, the hot ointment that he used to rub on his pitching arm to take the tightness out of his muscles, and filled a hypodermic syringe with it, then injected some of the ointment into his tube of toothpaste. Lyle then placed the toothpaste tube back in his locker.

Not long after, Lyle was sitting in the dressing room when Yogi, dressed in a T-shirt and shorts, came in with his toothbrush. He strode over to Lyle's locker, helped himself to the tube of toothpaste, squeezed out some onto his brush, and walked off toward the bathroom.

A few minutes later, the locker room was filled with the sound of Berra screaming. "My gums! My gums! Whooooooooooooooeeee! My gums are on fire!"

Lyle nodded. "They were smoking," he said with a grin.

When Bill Virdon succeeded Houk as Yankee manager in 1974, Lyle's reputation as a prankster was well established. He was bold enough by that time to make Virdon the target for one of his tricks.

Virdon was celebrating his birthday, and the club management presented him with a canvas chair that had his name blazoned across the back. Virdon scarcely had time to put the chair together before Lyle took a hacksaw and sawed it in two. "I left it lying in pieces in a heap," said Lyle.

The angry Virdon called a team meeting. "I got a birthday present today, and I really liked it," Virdon said. "It was a chair with my name on it, which somebody cut in half. I have a pretty good idea who did it." At that point, Virdon looked right at Lyle.

Lyle had been expecting to be accused of the prank. To throw Virdon off the track, he had hung the hacksaw in pitcher Rudy May's locker. The locker was near the spot where Virdon always stood when he held meetings.

After he had looked at Lyle, Virdon turned and saw the hacksaw in May's locker. May saw it, too. "It wasn't me! It wasn't me!" May cried out. "But I know who did it and I can tell you."

Then Virdon said, "I'm getting another chair. And it better not be cut." End of meeting.

Shortly after, Virdon did get a second replacement chair. But he never dared assemble it.

The rookie player drills his first home run in the major leagues. As he rounds the bases, the crowd's cheers ringing in his ears, he wears a wide grin. This is a moment he has dreamed of all his life. He is on cloud nine.

He touches home plate and heads for the dugout, knowing a hearty welcome awaits him. But no one claps him on the back. No one shakes his hand. His teammates are just sitting there silently, some gazing out toward the field, others staring down at the dugout floor. The manager is checking the lineup card. The poor rookie doesn't know what to think.

Then suddenly his teammates erupt, laughing and hollering. They pound him on the back. There are high fives all around. The Silent Treatment is over. The rookie is now "one of the guys."

In days past, rookies were often the victims of terrible tricks. The Silent Treatment, for example, could go on for weeks, and there was nothing good-natured about it. The veterans were a tight-knit group. They resented rookies; they looked upon them as intruders.

Rookies are still the targets of veterans' practical jokes, but they are not tinged with malice, as they once were. A rookie may enter the clubhouse to find his bags packed and placed near the door. That's typical.

Fernando Valenzuela, one of the most celebrated rookies of recent years, occasionally found himself the butt of pranksters' jokes. One day after a game, Valenzuela was in the shower washing his hair. He closed his eyes tight as he began rinsing out the shampoo. Jay Johnstone, a Dodger outfielder at the time, sneaked into the shower room alongside Valenzuela, and began pouring more shampoo on top of his head. The more vigorously Valenzuela rinsed, the more Johnstone poured, and the more suds formed. Finally, after several minutes of rinsing, Valenzuela got wise.

Mark (The Bird) Fidrych was the victim of an elaborate practical joke during his rookie season. As he was reaching the peak of his popularity that year, Fidrych was interviewed on national television following a "Game-of-the-Week" broadcast. During the interview, The Bird happened to let slip a couple of swear words. The next afternoon when he arrived at the ball park, a telegram was waiting for him. It read:

THIS IS TO INFORM YOU THAT YOU ARE
HEREBY FINED $250 FOR USING PROFANITY
ON THE NBC–TV GAME–OF–THE–WEEK TV SHOW.
SUCH CONDUCT WILL NOT BE TOLERATED.
ANY FURTHER SUCH ACTION COULD RESULT IN
YOUR SUSPENSION

SIGNED: BOWIE KUHN, COMMISSIONER

It looked exactly like a real telegram. It came in the standard Western Union envelope. After Fidrych read it, he leaped to his feet and rushed to the office of Tiger manager Ralph Houk.

"Look at this! Look at this!" Fidrych screamed. "They can't do this to me, can they?"

Houk was grim-faced. "I'm afraid they can," he said.

"This is awful," said Fidrych as he paced back and forth in the clubhouse, showing the telegram to anyone who would look at it. "I don't make that much money."

The players let Fidrych fume for about ten minutes. Then someone told him the telegram was a joke, that it had been typed up by a reporter in the press box and planted in his locker by one of his teammates. Fidrych was so relieved he forgot about getting angry.

Not every rookie or every player becomes the target of the

As a rookie, Mark Fidrych was victim of Detroit jokesters.

practical joker. On most teams, there is an inner circle of perpetrators and victims. Rex Kern was frequently on the receiving end of stunts pulled by Gaylord Perry when the two were Cleveland Indian teammates. Perry would tie Kern's uniform in knots and rip his best dress shorts into shreds. But Perry ignored many of the other Indian players. Kern once asked Perry why he singled him out as a victim so frequently. Perry replied, "Because I really like you, Kerny." Kern, a wild and crazy guy himself, understood.

Topps Chewing Gum, the principal manufacturer of baseball bubble gum cards, has been a target of baseball's practical jokers. The most famous stunt victimizing Topps occurred in 1958. The

Lou Burdette posed as a southpaw for this now famous baseball card.

Milwaukee Braves won the National League pennant that year, and carried the Yankee to seven games in the World Series before losing.

Southpaw Warren Spahn, who was to win election to the Hall of Fame, and a hard-throwing right-hander named Lou Burdette were the leading pitchers on the Milwaukee staff. They also led the team in antic behavior.

During the spring of 1958, when the Topps photographer visited the Milwaukee training camp to take photos of the players for the cards that would be issued the following winter, Burdette and Spahn decided to have some fun with him. With Spahn

This really isn't Aurelio Rodriquez; it's the Angels' batboy.

encouraging him, Burdette posed as a left-hander by putting his glove, which he normally wore on his left hand, on his right hand. He managed to conceal the fact that it was a glove meant to be worn on the left hand when the photo was taken. The experts at Topps didn't catch on to the gag until it was too late.

Today, the 1959 Topps Lou Burdette card (No. 440 in the set), depicting Burdette as a southpaw, is highly prized among collectors.

What has become another well-known deception took place in 1968. The batboy for the California Angels fooled the Topps photographer that year by posing in the place of Aurelio Rodriguez,

PHILLIES

Grant Jackson   PITCHER

Jackson's prank was to wear a batting glove on his pitching hand.

the team's third baseman. No one spotted the error until the card was in circulation.

Many of the pranks that have been played on the trusting photographers from Topps have involved gloves. Pitcher Grant Jackson of the Phillies managed to get himself photographed in a pitching pose for his 1970 card while wearing a batting glove on his pitching hand.

Steve Huntz, the Padres shortstop, was shown making a fielding play while wearing a batting glove for his 1970 card.

Pitcher Steve Hamilton, who was widely known as a flake, posed for his 1968 card while wearing a first baseman's mitt.

Pitcher Steve Hamilton grins because he fooled the photographer.

Joe Koppe, an infielder with the Angels, posed with his glove on the "wrong" hand in 1964. And Chris Speier, the flashy Expos shortstop, is pictured on his 1979 card while fielding a ground ball, but with his glove on his throwing hand.

Pitcher Tommy John of the White Sox appears in the follow-through stage of his delivery on his 1969 card. Oddly, the ball is still in his glove.

A very common trick is to represent yourself as a right-handed batter when you're really a leftie, or a left-handed batter when you're actually a rightie. Gene Freese pulled this stunt three times, first in 1962 as a member of the Reds, in 1965 when a

Right-hand batter Gene Freeze liked to pose as a leftie.

Pirate, and again in 1966 when he played for the White Sox.

Others who are pictured batting the "wrong" way on their Topps cards are Clete Boyer of the Yankees (in 1962), Bob Uecker of the Cards (1965), Jim Fregosi of the Angels (1967), Gary Geiger of the Astros (1969), and Mack Jones of the Expos (1969).

"They're always trying things," says Mickey Palmer, a Topps photographer for many years. "You have to keep alert, know whether a guy is a right-handed batter or a leftie, and know whether he throws right-handed or left-handed. But sometimes you get tricked. They usually catch the mistakes at the office, but once in a while one slips through."

6

Stunts

Players who are just plain wacky are responsible for most of baseball's craziness. But there is also a fair amount of insanity involving players that is planned in advance. It is the type of zaniness that rises out of stunts dreamed up by team owners and their publicity people.

The most famous stunt of this kind has been recounted many times, but no book that concerns baseball wackiness would be complete without mentioning it.

On August 19, 1951, in the first inning of the second game of a doubleheader between the St. Louis Browns and the Detroit Tigers, manager Zack Taylor of the Browns sent Eddie Gaedel up to bat for right fielder Frank Saucier. Saucier is little remembered today. But Gaedel's name has become a baseball legend.

Gaedel was smaller than all but the smallest of Little Leaguers. He stood 3-foot-7; he weighed 65 pounds. Eddie Gaedel was a midget, the only midget ever to play major league baseball.

The idea of having a midget play for a big league team sprung from the fertile mind of Bill Veeck, owner of the Browns, one of the pitiful teams in baseball. Few people ever attended their games. In 1951, the American League was celebrating its fiftieth anniversary. Veeck, who had a long career as a promoter, and believed it was the duty of an owner to entertain the fans who paid their way into the park, decided it would be a good idea to throw a party to celebrate the anniversary. It would be staged between games of a Sunday doubleheader against the last-place Detroit Tigers. The Browns themselves were next to last in the standings.

Veeck and his associates began mapping plans. Entertaining in the infield would be a juggler, a trampoline act, and a balancing act. A band would seranade the fans from home plate. Max Patkin, the well-known clown, would be hired for the day. A parade of old-fashioned cars would circle the infield and everyone who bought a ticket would receive a piece of birthday cake and a slice of ice cream.

Veeck kept secret his idea of sending a midget up to bat. He did, however, tell Zack Taylor, the manager of the Browns, and Bob Fishel, the St. Louis publicity man (who is now assistant to the president of the American League). Veeck also told his wife.

Veeck called an agent who had booked acts for him in the past and asked him to find a midget, someone who was a bit athletic and would be willing to go along with a gag. The booking agent found Eddie Gaedel in Chicago and sent him to see Veeck.

"How would you like to be a big league ball player?" Veeck asked him.

Eddie didn't think too much of the idea. "You'll be the only midget in the history of the game," Veeck said. "You'll be appearing before thousands of people. Your name will go into the record books for all time. You'll become famous, Eddie." After Veeck's sales talk, Eddie began to think it might be fun.

Veeck handed Eddie a toy bat and asked him to demonstrate his batting stance. He instructed him to go into a deep crouch, so his strike zone would be as small as possible. (The rules of baseball say that the strike zone is between the batter's armpits and the top of his knees.) When Eddie went into his crouch, Veeck took a ruler and measured his strike zone. It was 1½ inches.

Veeck instructed Eddie that he was not to swing at the ball during the game. "All you have to do is stand there and take four balls," Veeck said. "Then you'll trot down to first base and we'll send in someone to run for you."

Getting a uniform for Eddie loomed as a problem, but then Veeck remembered that the seven-year-old son of the club's vice president had his Browns' uniform hanging in the locker room. It would be perfect for Eddie. Veeck gave instructions to have the number ⅛ sewn on the back of the uniform.

The day before his appearance, Eddie signed an official contract. Veeck had agreed to pay him $100 for the day. A copy of the contract was mailed to league headquarters Saturday night. Because there was no mail delivery on Sunday, Veeck knew it would not arrive until the following day. By then, the stunt would be history.

Another copy of the contract was given to Zack Taylor. This was to show the umpires in case Eddie's status as a "real" player was questioned.

More than 18,000 fans showed up on the day the stunt was planned. Veeck was thrilled. It was the biggest crowd to see the Browns at home in four years.

After the first game, which the Browns lost, the celebration began. Eddie, in full uniform, was put inside the hollowed-out section of a huge birthday cake, and the cake was wheeled out onto the field. At the appropriate moment, the public-address announcer declared: "Ladies and gentlemen, as a special birthday present to manager Zack Taylor, the management is presenting him with a brand-new Brownie." Out popped Eddie from the cake.

Some grins and mild applause greeted him. Most people thought the gag was over. Only a handful of insiders knew what was to come.

The second game of the doubleheader got underway. The Tigers went down in order in the top half of the inning.

As the Browns prepared to bat in the bottom half of the inning, Eddie emerged from the dugout swinging three little bats. The public-address announcer said: "For the Browns, number one-eighth, Eddie Gaedel, batting for Saucier."

Eddie tossed aside two of the bats and started for home plate. The fans could hardly believe their eyes.

Ed Hurley, the umpire at home plate, was not amused by Veeck's prank. He shouted out to Zack Taylor, "Hey, what's going on here?" Taylor pretended nothing was wrong. He showed Hurley Gaedel's contract and other documents that had been provided by Veeck. Hurley had no choice but to wave Gaedel into the batter's box. The fans went wild.

Bob Swift, the Detroit catcher, realizing that the situation called for special strategy, went out to the mound to confer with pitcher Bobby Cain. When he returned, and Gaedel stepped up to the plate, Swift got down on both knees in order to be able to offer Cain a low enough target.

Midget Eddie Gaedel at bat for the St. Louis Browns

Gaedel spread his feet wide apart, cocked his little bat high, and eyed the pitcher. It was a very serious moment for him.

Cain started out as if he were facing a batter of conventional size, and the first pitch was a fastball that sailed past Eddie's head. The second pitch was the same.

As Cain got set to deliver a third time, he was laughing so hard he could barely throw. Ball three and ball four were merely lobs that sailed high above Eddie's head.

Eddie tossed aside his bat and trotted down to first base. The fans were rolling in the aisles. Zack Taylor sent in Jim Delsing to run for Eddie.

The St. Louis dugout was on the third base side of the field, which meant that Eddie had to cut across the infield to make his exit. As he did so, he stopped several times to raise a hand or wave his cap in acknowledgment of the crowd's cheers.

Veeck was hardly prepared for what happened the next day. League officials and many baseball writers blasted him for what he had done. These men looked upon baseball as if it were some kind of a religion. Veeck, by sending a midget up to bat during a game, had committed some kind of a sacrilege, they said.

Veeck shrugged off the criticism. But he became angered when he learned that American League president Will Harridge had ordered that Eddie's name be removed from baseball's official records.

Veeck wouldn't stand for that. He pointed out to Harridge that Gaedel had signed an official league contract and had been permitted an official time at bat in an official game that had been supervised by a league umpire.

If Gaedel were not to be permitted an official time at bat, then how could one explain the pitches that Cain had thrown to him? And how could one explain that Saucier had left the game for a pinch hitter, or that Delsing had entered the game as a pinch runner? Not including Gaedel's at-bat in the official records, said Veeck, would cast doubts on the integrity of all of baseball's records.

In the end, reason prevailed. Eddie's name went into the record book. It remains there to this day.

Eddie's career in baseball, however, was brought to an abrupt end. The American League office refused to approve his contract, saying that "his participation in American League games is not in the best interest of baseball."

That didn't matter to Eddie. His services were suddenly in great demand as a result of the publicity he had recieved, and

Veeck was able to book him for appearances that netted him several thousands of dollars.

Veeck used Eddie a couple of more times in ensuing years. Once, when Veeck owned the Chicago White Sox, he employed Eddie and two other midgets to dress in weird clothing that was supposed to make them look like Martians (gold helmets, coveralls, and shoes, plus oxygen tanks). A helicopter landed the trio behind second base at Comiskey Park, whereupon they "captured" Chicago's smallish second base combination of Nelson Fox and Luis Aparicio. The public-address system announced that the Martians had arrived to assist Fox and Aparicio "in their battle against the giant earthlings."

Eddie died in 1961. Some people say that he deserves enshrinement in the Hall of Fame. After all, they point out, he was the central figure in what is generally regarded as the zaniest moment in all of baseball history.

In 1949, two years before the mischief involving Eddie Gaedel, the Browns were involved in another unusual promotion stunt. While it didn't have the gleeful quality of Eddie's turn at bat, it's worth recalling because of its novelty.

This was a pitcher-an-inning stunt. At the beginning of each inning, the Browns brought in a new pitcher.

The game that featured this goofiness was offered on the last day of the season. The seventh-place Browns trailed the Yankees and Red Sox, who were tied for the league lead, by 43½ games. (There were only eight teams in the American League at the time, and they were not divided into divisions.) The Browns faced the sixth-place Chicago White Sox, who were 33½ games behind the league leaders. It is safe to say it was not a crucial game.

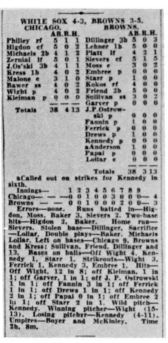

WHITE SOX 4-3, BROWNS 3-5.

CHICAGO.	AB.R.H.	BROWNS.		AB.R.H.
Philley rf	5 1 1	Dillinger 3b		5 0 3
Higdon cf	5 0 2	Lehner 1b		5 0 0
Michaels 2b	4 1 2	Platt lf		4 2 1
Zernial lf	5 0 1	Sievers cf		5 1 5
J.Os'ski 3b	4 1 1	Moss c		3 0 2
Kress 1b	4 0 2	Embree p		0 0 0
Malone c	3 1 0	Starr p		1 0 0
Bawer ss	4 0 2	Kokos rf		4 0 0
Wight p	4 0 2	Friend 2b		5 0 0
Kleiman p	0 0 0	Sullivan ss		3 0 2
		Garver p		0 0 0
Totals	38 4 13	J.P.Ostrow-ski p		0 0 0
		Fannin p		1 0 0
		Ferrick p		0 0 0
		Drews p		1 0 0
		Kennedy p		0 0 0
		aAnderson		1 0 0
		Papai p		0 0 0
		Lollar c		0 0 0
		Totals		38 3 13

aCalled out on strikes for Kennedy in sixth.

Innings—	1 2 3 4 5 6 7 8 9	
Chicago—	— —0 0 1 0 0 3 0 0 0—	4
Browns —	— 0 0 1 0 0 0 2 0 0—	3

Errors—none. Runs batted in—Higdon, Moss, Baker 3, Sievers 2. Two-base hits—Higdon 2, Baker. Home run—Sievers. Stolen base—Dillinger. Sacrifice—Lollar. Double plays—Baker, Michaels Lollar. Left on bases—Chicago 9, Browns and Kress; Sullivan, Friend, Dillinger and 13. Bases on balls—Off Wight 4, Kennedy 1, Starr 1. Strikeouts—Wight 3, Ferrick 1, Kennedy 3, Embree 1. Hits—Off Wight, 12 in 8; off Kleiman, 1 in 1; off Garver, 1 in 1; off J. P. Ostrowski 1 in 1; off Fannin 3 in 1; off Ferrick 1 in 1; off Drews 1 in 1; off Kennedy 2 in 1; off Papai 0 in 1; off Embree 2 in 1; off Starr 2 in 1. Wild pitch—Kennedy. Winning pitcher—Wight (15-13). Losing pitcher—Kennedy (4-11). Umpires—Boyer and McKinley. Time 2h. 8m.

Box score is stuffed with pitchers' names following Browns' pitcher-an-inning stunt.

Ned Garver started for St. Louis. After hurling one inning, Garver was replaced by Joe Ostrowski.

Cliff Fannin pitched the third inning, to be followed in successive innings by Tom Ferrick, Karl Drews, Bill Kennedy, Al Papai, Red Embree, and Dick Starr.

Seven of the Browns' hurlers pitched scoreless innings. But Fannin gave up a run in the third, Kennedy was tagged with the loss after the White Sox pounded him for three runs in the sixth, as the Browns went down to defeat, 4–2.

The game served to establish a record for the number of pitchers used by one team in one game. Otherwise, it has all but been forgotten. Except for a box score, the *St. Louis Post Dispatch* did not even mention the contest.

Did the stunt have any value? Of course it did. Advance notice of it served to attract 9,847 fans, one of the Browns' biggest crowds of the season.

Bill Veeck, the owner who dreamed up the stunt involving midget Eddie Gaedel, is regarded as baseball's greatest promotion genius. But during the 1960s and 1970s, Veeck was often rivaled by Charlie Finley, who owned the Kansas City A's. (The club moved to Oakland in 1968.)

When based in Kansas City, the A's were seldom a contending team, so Finley staged stunts for the very reason Bill Veeck did—to boost attendance. Once, when the Kansas City starting lineup was being introduced, the players rode into the park by mule train. (The team's mascot happened to be a mule.) Another time, the players arrived by chauffeured limousine. And when slugger Rocky Colovito was nearing his 300th career home run, Finley had a Brink's armored truck park behind the left field wall. He announced it contained the cash with which he intended to reward Rocky.

It was Finley, incidentally, who triggered a revolution in uniform fashions. It used to be that all uniforms were the same, white at home, gray on the road. In 1962, Finley put his Kansas City Athletics in colorful green and gold uniforms.

The Kansas City players were hooted at by other teams. Many observers expected the team would revert to the traditional uniforms, but Finley would not back down. Although virtually all teams remained in white and gray throughout the 1960s, the idea of color-coordinated uniforms eventually took hold.

What was one of Finley's most notable promotion stunts took

place on September 8, 1965. The A's were playing the California Angels in Kansas City.

It was Dagoberto (Campy) Campaneris night. The team's slim, 25-year-old shortstop, then in his second season with the A's, was to become the first player in major league history to play all nine positions in one game.

The stunt produced mixed blessings for the A's. A crowd of 21,576 paid their way into Municipal Stadium to watch Campaneris, and that was considered a good turnout for the A's during that period. Unfortunately, the A's lost the game.

Nor was the night an unqualified success for Campaneris. Yes, he did achieve what he set out to achieve. But an error he made led to one California run and his ragged pitching to another. And in the ninth inning, when he was catching, Campy suffered a shoulder and neck injury in a collision at home plate, and was out of the lineup for several days as a result.

The early innings were uneventful. Campaneris started the game at shortstop, his normal position. He switched over to second base in the second inning and was credited with an assist when he handled the ball in a rundown.

At third base in the third inning, he had no chances. But he caught a fly ball in left field in the fourth inning and repeated the play in center field in the fifth inning.

He had trouble in right field in the sixth inning. With two out and a man on first, Jim Fregosi lofted a high fly to right center field. Campaneris managed to get under the ball, but it caromed off the heel of his glove, and the runner on first scored on the error. That boosted the Angels into a 2–1 lead.

The game calmed down in the seventh inning. Playing first base, Campy had one putout.

As the Kansas City pitcher in the eighth inning, Campy had

more difficulties. Jose Cardenal, the first batter to face him, popped out. But then Campy walked Albie Pearson and Fregosi on eight straight pitches. He pitched two more balls before giving up a single to Joe Adcock, with Pearson scoring on the play.

Campaneris then bore down and retired the next two batters. The score was now 3–1, Angels.

For the ninth inning, Campy went behind the plate. The Angels immediately created some problems for him. After Ed Kirkpatrick singled, he stole second. Tom Egan walked. Paul Schall flied out, with Kirkpatrick taking third.

Suddenly the Angels sprung a double steal. Egan raced for second and the 200-pound Kirkpatrick came thundering down the line toward home plate.

Campy threw to Dick Green at second, and Green threw back to Campy in an effort to cut off the run. Campy gloved the ball, then whirled to meet Kirkpatrick, who barrelled into him. The two men went sprawling, but Campy held onto the ball and Kirkpatrick was out.

Campaneris was hurt—and angry. He jumped to his feet and raised his fists, ready to wade into Kirkpatrick. But the two men were separated before any blows were struck.

Campaneris, in obvious pain, had to leave the game. When the A's rallied for two runs to tie matters in the bottom of the ninth, Campy was on the way to the hospital for X-rays. The A's ultimately lost the game in thirteen innings, 5–3.

On September 22, 1968, Campaneris' feat was repeated by Cesar Tovar of the Minnesota Twins. The Oakland A's furnished the opposition. The Twins won, 2–1.

Tovar opened the game as the Minnesota pitcher. Ironically, Campaneris was the first batter he faced. Campy fouled out.

Campaneris enjoyed a long and successful career. In 1965,

Yankees signed Campaneris in 1983, hailing him for his versatility.

the same year he played all the positions in a game, he led the American League in stolen bases. He was also the league's leading thief in 1967, 1968, 1970, and 1972.

The A's traded Campy to California in 1976, and he was dealt to Texas in 1980. He played in Mexico in 1982. But a year later, he was back in the major leagues, this time with the New York Yankees.

In the seasons following the Campaneris stunt, Finley continued to act as a mischief-maker, often causing discomfort among baseball's old-line owners. But Finley's stunts never made the Kansas City team a success in terms of attendance. So after the 1967 season, Finley pulled up stakes and moved the A's to Oakland. There the A's attracted fans in a manner that put a smile on Finley's face. They did it by relying on a tried and proven "gimmick"—they won consistently.

Another stunt based upon lineup tinkering took place in 1963. This time the team involved was the Houston Colts.

Yes, the *Colts*, not the Astros.

When Houston joined the National League in 1962, the owners called the team the Houston Colt .45s, after the famous gun. But the fans called them the Houston Colts, after horses, not guns. And just plain Colts they became.

The Colt name lasted for just two seasons. In the final Colt game, played at Colt Stadium on September 27, 1963, the Colts fielded baseball's first all-rookie lineup. It was made up of these players:

Brock Davis, left field
Jimmy Wynn, center field
Aaron Pointer, right field
Rusty Staub, first base
Joe Morgan, second base
Glenn Vaughan, third base
Sonny Jackson, shortstop
Jerry Grote, catcher
Jay Dahl, pitcher

The players averaged 19 years, 4 months in age. It was believed to be the youngest team ever to take the field in a major league game. *The Sporting News* called the squad the Colt Kiddie Corps.

Starting pitcher Jay Dahl, a chunky left-hander from California, was 17. He thus became the youngest pitcher to start a major league game since Joe Nuxhall had the honor in 1945. Nuxhall was 15 years old when he started for the Cincinnati Reds.

Cot Deal, the Colt pitching coach, said Dahl was surprisingly calm in the clubhouse before the game. "But," said Deal, "he did ask me if I could suggest something for sweaty hands."

The inexperience of the Colt rookies was apparent, and they lost to the Mets, 10–3. Dahl, who left the game after three innings, was the losing pitcher.

The next year, 1964, Houston moved into baseball's first indoor stadium, the Astrodome, and the Colts became the Astros.

While the Colt name was not long remembered, several of the players who were members of the club's 1963 rookie lineup were heard from time and time again in the years that followed. Such players as Sonny Jackson, Rusty Staub, Jerry Grote, Jimmy Wynn, and Joe Morgan carved out splendid careers. Morgan, in fact, who enjoyed an All-Star career with the Cincinnati Reds and appeared in the 1983 World Series as the second baseman for the Philadelphia Phillies, was mentioned often as a Hall of Fame candidate.

One last piece of staged wackiness that must be mentioned involves not an entire lineup, but just one player. And the player happens to be one of the greatest hitters in baseball history— Stan Musial.

A St. Louis Cardinal throughout a career that spanned two decades, Musial, an outfielder, won seven batting championships, the last one in 1957 when he was 37 years old. The National League's Most Valuable Player three times, Musial hit .300 or better in 17 of 21 seasons. His 3,630 hits put him forth on the

Stan Musial, one of the greatest hitters in baseball history, had a one-pitch pitching career.

all-time hit list behind Ty Cobb, Pete Rose, and Hank Aaron.

Once in his long and brilliant career, Musial made an appearance as a pitcher. It took place on September 28, 1952, the final day of the season. The Cards were playing the Chicago Cubs.

Musial and Frankie Baumholtz of the Cubs were locked in a duel for the National League batting championship at the time. Musial was hitting .336, and Baumholtz .326.

In the first inning, after St. Louis starting pitcher Harvey Haddix had walked lead-off batter Tommy Brown, Baumholtz came to bat, and Musial was brought in from center field to pitch to him. (Haddix went out to play right field, and right fielder Hal Rice moved over to center.)

Musial, a left-hander, knew something about pitching, for he had pitched for Daytona Beach in the Florida State League in 1940. He took only a couple of warm-up throws.

Baumholtz stepped up to the plate. Musial fired a fastball. Baumholtz swung and rapped the ball on a big hop to Solly Hemus at third base.

Hemus, figuring he'd start a double play, fumbled the ball, and then threw too late to first base. It was scored an error.

Baumholtz would have had a 5-for-5 day to overtake Musial (who would had to have gone hitless). The error, since it counted as a time at bat, assured that Baumholtz would not be perfect that day, and Musial would win the batting crown, his third straight.

That was it. Musial's career as a pitcher lasted one pitch. After throwing to Baumholtz, Musial returned to center field. (Rice went back to center field, and Haddix took over on the mound again.)

Musial banged out a solid hit to center field in the ninth inning. He was 1-for-3 for the afternoon, .336 for the season. Baumholtz's 1-for-4 day dropped him to .325. The Cubs won the game, 3–0.

The stunt, of course, has been given recognition in baseball's official records. On the full page devoted to Musial and his hitting achievements, there are these lines of type:

PITCHING RECORD

Year	Club	League	G	IP	W	L	Pct.	H	R	SO	BB	ERA
1952	St. Louis	National	1	0	0	0	.000	0	0	0	0	0.00

(7)

Men in Blue and Gray

To players and fans alike, there is nothing funny about being an umpire. It is one of the toughest and least-appreciated jobs in sports.

In the average game, the four umpires are involved in 60 to 80 safe-or-out decisions. The umpire behind home plate must rule on some 250 to 300 ball-and-strike calls.

All the while, the umpire must control the game, never letting it get out of hand. "A good umpire," Casey Stengel once said, "gives every player confidence. He knows he is going to get justice."

To be an umpire, it takes keen eyesight and the ability to make split-second judgments, qualities the players, managers, and fans often question.

Umpires work in four-man crews that live together during the season. They are not allowed to travel on the chartered planes the teams use nor are they allowed to fraternize with the players at any time. It is a lonely life. Much of an umpire's time is spent watching television or reading novels in hotel rooms.

Umpiring is a profession in which one works relatively unknown. For many years, Dolly Stark was one of the best umpires in the National League, then he quit abruptly. "I'm sick of being in a public profession," he said, "in which the greatest compliment I can receive is the silence of the crowd. An umpire can work a perfect game, call every play right, and get by without a beef, and not a fan can tell you his name ten minutes after the game."

Despite the rigors of the job and the fact that they're practically nameless, umpires have been involved in some of baseball's funniest moments. This is not to say there are any jokesters out there, but a handful have been colorful or temperamental, and a good number became noted for their clever banter and quick wit.

Here are some examples.

Tim Hurst was not only an outstanding umpire in baseball's early days, but one of the most noted figures in sports. He refereed fights and promoted the six-day bicycle races at Madison Square Garden.

As an umpire, Hurst fell into the habit of calling out runners at first before the ball reached the first baseman's mitt. Players on the Philadelphia Athletics plotted to expose what Hurst was doing.

The A's were playing the Washington Senators and comfortably ahead. A slow-footed Senator batter hit an easy grounder to Eddie Collins at second base. Collins made a throwing motion toward first, but held onto the ball. First baseman Harry Davis pretended to catch the phantom throw. Hurst called the runner out.

Immediately, the Washington first base coach yelled at Hurst, "Davis hasn't got the ball!" Then Collins opened his glove to show he still had it.

The moment that he realized he had been made a fool of, Hurst boiled with rage. The madder he got, the more the A's laughed. Even the Washington players joined in. Hurst focused his anger on Collins. He called the second baseman an assortment of unpretty names. When Collins approached Hurst, perhaps to apologize to him, the umpire spit in his face.

Ban Johnson, the president of the American League, suspended Hurst and ordered an investigation of the incident. A Philadephia newspaper pointed out that Collins was a college graduate (a rarity among ballplayers in those days) and that Hurst's conduct toward him would discourage other young men of good manners and good breeding from entering professional baseball. Influenced by the newspaper article, Johnson fired Hurst.

Afterward Hurst shrugged off the incident, saying, "I never did like them college boys."

Johnny Temple, second baseman for the Cincinnati Reds, was a solid fielder and adequate hitter, but no star. Larry Goetz once tossed him out of a game after he had hotly protested a called strike.

Afterward, Temple sought out Goetz. "How come you let those other guys argue," Temple asked, "but threw me out?"

Goetz had a ready answer. "I don't mind when the lions and tigers get on me," he said, "but when the nits and gnats start in, it's too much."

Tough-talking Bill Guthrie, an umpire for more than forty years, was well known for the fairness of his decisions and quick wit.

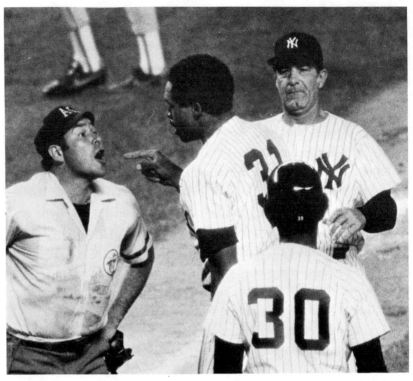

Umpire Al Clark stands his ground as Yankee Dave Winfield sounds off.

A noted example of his use of both occurred following a third-strike call in an American Association game with young Hack Wilson at the plate. Livid with rage, Wilson demonstrated his dissatisfaction with Guthrie's decision by flipping his bat high into the air. Guthrie removed his mask and eyed the bat as it sailed upward.

"Son," he said softly, "if that bat comes down you're out of the game."

On another day, Jimmy Dykes, a nonstop umpire baiter, disputed a called strike when he was at bat.

"Keep your mouth shut," Guthrie told him, "and nobody but me, you, and the catcher will know you can't see anymore."

One afternoon in Boston, Guthrie cleared the Red Sox bench of troublemakers who had been riding him unmercifully throughout the afternoon. When he returned to his position behind the plate, Guthrie spotted Charlie (Heine) Wagner at his third base post.

"You're out of the game, too," he shouted to Heine.

"Me?" the coach said. "I didn't say anything."

"No, you didn't," Guthrie agreed, "but you were thinking."

Now Wagner was angry. "How do you know I was thinking?" he snarled.

"I don't know," said Guthrie. "But I'll give you credit for it anyway. Get out!"

Cal Hubbard used to tell batters, "Boys, I'm one of those umpires who can make a mistake on the close ones. So if it's close, you'd better hit it."

Angelo Guglielmo was one of the most noted minor league umpires of all time. Although he stood only 5-foot-3, he was a tyrant on the field, setting records for ejecting players and managers wherever he happened to be working. In 1952, the only year he worked in the major leagues, Guglielmo won notoriety as being the first umpire to throw Jackie Robinson out of a game.

Guglielmo is also remembered as the only umpire in the history of baseball to change a ball-strike call. It happened when Guglielmo was umpiring in the International League toward the end of his career. Syracuse's Steve Bilko came to the plate. Bilko, like Guglielmo, was a minor league veteran, and so the two knew each other well.

The count was one ball, one strike. Bilko took the next pitch. "Strike two!" Guglielmo cried.

Bilko's brow furrowed. He stepped out of the batter's box, turned toward Guglielmo, and said, "Gugie, how long have you been umpiring?"

Guglielmo looked at the big slugger quizzically. He didn't like conversation between pitches. It held up the game. But Bilko was a long-time acquaintance, so he answered him. "Twenty-six years," he said. "Why do you want to know?"

"Because," said Bilko, stepping back into the batter's box, "I've been watching you work for fifteen of those years, and that's the only pitch I've ever seen you miss."

"*Time!*" Guglielmo screamed, and he threw both hands into the air, stopping play. Then he turned around, cupped his mouth with his hands, and shouted up to the official scorer sitting in the press box, "That's ball two!" The scorer, though puzzled, nodded.

Guglielmo stood to one side and waited until the count had been changed on the scoreboard, then he took up his position behind the plate again. When Bilko stepped up again, Guglielmo announced to him, "Now, I'm perfect."

Umpires never like to reverse decisions, but umpire Ron Luciano once had to change a home run call. It happened several years ago in a game between the Orioles and Angels in Baltimore. California's Tommy Harper blasted a long drive down the left field foul line. It was up to Luciano to decide whether the ball was fair or foul. He started running down the line toward the stands, watching the ball as he ran, trying to follow it. But it was difficult. The sun was reflecting off the glass windows of the

Umpire Ron Luciano saw the play, but was temporarily blinded by his hat in Milwaukee-Toronto game in 1977.

press box and Luciano lost the ball in the glare. He had no idea where it came down.

Luciano had been taught at umpires' school always to make a call. That, he was told, was the first rule of umpiring—right or wrong, always make a call.

Luciano happened to glance at Baltimore left fielder Don Baylor, and saw he was looking at the seats. The Baltimore crowd was quiet, as if something bad had happened to their team. Luciano figured that the ball must have been a home run.

He leaped high into the air and twirled one hand to indicate the ball was fair. Immediately all hell broke loose. Don Baylor came charging toward him. The Oriole pitchers in the bullpen climbed over the fence and came racing his way. Third baseman Brooks Robinson, known for his mild manner, was enraged. Then Luciano saw manager Earl Weaver leading the rest of the Oriole team out of the dugout, and they were headed his way. Meanwhile, the Oriole fans were screaming.

Luciano realized he had made a mistake—a big one. He hurried across the field to consult with Bill Haller, umpire at first.

"I blew it, huh?" said Luciano.

Haller shrugged. "Only by forty or fifty feet," he said.

Billy Evans was an outstanding American League umpire for more than a quarter of a century. Thanks to a calm and gentlemanly manner, he rarely had problems with even the most troublesome players and managers.

Evans would listen to a protest patiently and never interrupt. Then, when the raging player or manager was beginning to run out of words, Evans would say: "You haven't said anything to make me feel I'm in error. So the ruling stands. Protest the game, if you care to, but let's resume play."

Luciano liked to have fun on the field, a trait that did not endear him to American League officials. One thing he liked to do was pick up the paper airplanes that fans would send soaring out of the stands and sail them back into the seats. One day at Anaheim Stadium, a fan lofted a paper airplane made from the page of the game program onto the field near where Luciano was standing. Luciano picked it up and was about to launch it back toward the stands when an article about a player he was friendly with caught his eye. Luciano began reading the article. As he was reading, the runner on first base tried to steal second. Luciano threw down the airplane as soon as he realized what was going on, but he was too late to get into position for the call.

"I called him out," said Luciano, "figuring I had a fifty-fifty chance of being right. No one argued, so I guess I got it right."

Emmett Ashford, who joined the American League's umpiring staff in 1966, was the Jackie Robinson of umpires, the first black umpire in the major leagues.

Ashford had a flamboyant umpiring style. He boomed out his calls with his strong voice. He put a little extra into his arm and hand motions. "I'm an extrovert and I couldn't help it," he told Larry Gerlach for his book, *The Men in Blue*. "I guess you might say I'm a natural-born ham."

Ashford knew when to be a showman and when not to be. When to be an *umpire*, not merely a black umpire. But he never sidestepped the issue of race. And, on more than a few occasions, he got some humor out of it.

One such incident occurred during an exhibition game in Arizona. A hitter took a half swing and Ashford called the pitch a ball. Leo Durocher charged out of the dugout to protest. As was usual on such calls, Ashford consulted the umpire at first

Emmett Ashford's distinctive style added to the fun of the games he umpired.

base. He agreed with Ashford that the batter had not taken a full swing; the pitch was a ball.

By now, Durocher was at home plate. "What have we got? What have we got?" Durocher was yelling.

Ashford stuck his face up against Durocher's and replied, "It was not a strike. And you have it in black and white—him and me at the plate." Durocher retreated to the dugout.

Few umpires ever commanded a game in the manner of big and explosive George Magerkurth. A one-time 240-pound professional football player and heavyweight boxer, Magerkurth had a stormy 18-year career in the National League. Quarrels, harsh words, and fistfights punctuated games that he worked. When a player or a manager protested one of his decisions, it was usual for Magerkurth to blast his antagonist from the field with a roar loud enough to be heard in the deepest reaches of the stands.

But Magerkurth is not remembered for the fiery way in which he controlled matters, but for a game in which he appeared to be completely tamed.

It happened at Ebbets Field in Brooklyn. The Dodgers had just lost a close game. A Brooklyn fan, blaming Magerkurth for the defeat, raced out onto the field just as the game ended and swarmed all over him. Although only about half Magerkurth's size, the fan knocked him to the ground and then began pounding him with his fists.

Police quickly broke up the skirmish, but not before a newspaper photographer took a picture of the two men. The next day newspapers across the country printed the photo. It showed the fan, sitting astride Magerkurth, beating him fiercely. Magerkurth was terribly embarrassed by the incident and never managed to live it down.

When Jimmy Dykes was with the Chicago White Sox, he once took a long lead off first base, then began daydreaming. A snap throw from the catcher woke him up. Desperately, he dived back to the base.

Before umpire Bill Dineen could make his call, Dykes began screaming, "I made it! I made it!"

Dineen, with his thumb indicating that Dykes was out, looked down at him and said, "You certainly did, Jimmy. But what detained you?"

(8)

All-time Wackos

It's not hard to pick a team composed of baseball wackos. There have been so many flaky players through the years that there are several candidates for each position and enough pitchers to staff several teams. What is difficult is choosing the wackiest wacko at each position. Anyway, here's an attempt:

FIRST BASE: MARV THRONEBERRY—There was never a more pitiful baseball team than the 1962 New York Mets. Made up of castoffs from other teams and inexperienced kids, the 1962 Mets managed to win only 40 games while losing 120.

It was not merely that the team lost a record number of games, it was the way in which they lost them. There was, for example, a 15-inning game against the Philadelphia Phillies in which Al Jackson went all the way, allowing only three hits, only to lose in the final inning on two errors at first base by Marv Throneberry.

When Throneberry's birthday came around later in the season, center fielder Richie Ashburn walked over to Throneberry's locker stall, shook his hand, congratulated him, and said, "We were going to give you a cake, Marv, but we were afraid you'd drop it."

There are countless stories that document Marvelous Marv's shortage of talent. He found many foolish and absurd ways to do harm to the hapless Mets. One time he booted a ground ball in the first inning of a game at the Polo Grounds, allowing an unearned run to score.

Marv came to bat in the bottom of the inning. As if to redeem himself for the error, he blasted a towering drive between outfielders. As the ball rolled toward the fence, Marv rounded first, thundered past second, and went sliding into third for a triple. The crowd cheered happily.

But the opposing team claimed that Marv had failed to touch second base. The umpire agreed. Marv was called out.

Manager Casey Stengel came rushing out of the Mets' dugout to protest. But before Stengel got a chance to present his argument to the umpire, the first base coach stopped him. "Don't bother, Casey," said the coach. "He didn't touch first, either."

SECOND BASE: HERMAN (GERMANY) SCHAEFER — During fifteen years in the major leagues in a career that ended in 1918, Germany Schaefer was a Cub, Tiger, Senator, Yankee, and Indian. He is remembered for his zany base running. He made a practice of stealing bases in reverse. Upon reaching second base, he would steal his way back to first, a move that was meant to upset the opposing pitcher. Schaefer did this so often that officials passed a rule making it mandatory to run the bases only in a counterclockwise direction.

Maranville, a good friend of Babe Ruth's, was nicknamed "Rabbit" for the way he bounded around.

SHORTSTOP: WALTER (RABBIT) MARANVILLE—Maranville got his nickname when a fan once noted, "Why, he bounces around like a rabbit." He stood only 5-foot-5 and never weighed more than 155 pounds. An infielder for the Boston Braves and several other National League clubs, Maranville's trademark was his vest-pocket catch. On any high pop fly, he would practically ignore the ball until the last possible moment, then trap it with both hands in front of his chest.

Maranville clowned around in every kind of situation. Once, when he was in a batting slump, he went up to hit with one out. Just before he stepped up to the plate, he suddenly cried out, "Two out!" tossed his bat away and returned to the dugout.

On another occasion, a pitcher kept trying to pick him off second base. At least half a dozen times, Maranville had to go sliding back. When the pitcher threw to second at yet another time, Maranville, to break the monotony, went scampering back between the umpire's legs and still managed to arrive safely.

If his own pitcher seemed to be stalling during a game, Maranville would lean against an imaginary wall behind the infield, and sag slowly until he collapsed on the ground. Upon hitting a high pop fly, the Rabbit would mount his bat as if it were a hobby horse and, screaming terrible threats, pursue the catcher who was pursuing the ball.

Maranville's rookie season was 1912. Twenty years later players and fans were still laughing at his antics. He retired in 1933.

THIRD BASE: DOUG RADER—Rader's wackiness is documented earlier in this book, in Chapter 2. Here's another story about him: Once, in a New York hotel, Rader was infuriated by a room-service bill for $18 that arrived along with four cheeseburgers and four Cokes that he and his roommate, Norm Miller, had ordered.

"I'm sorry, sir," said the waiter, "but if you send them back, they'll still charge you."

Rader and Miller ate their food. Afterward, Rader was still upset. He wrapped the dishes, glasses, ketchup bottle, salt and pepper shakers, and the leftovers into the tablecloth and tied it in a bundle. He carried the bundle to the elevator, placed it on the floor inside, and sent it down to the lobby.

CATCHER: BOB UECKER—From 1962 through 1967, Uecker was a backup catcher for three teams, the Braves, Cards, and Phillies. He was, by the most generous estimates, a mediocre player, but while he may have lacked in talent, he was a Hall of Famer when it came to quips and high jinks.

Uecker's lifetime batting average is precisely .200. Once during an appearance on the Johnny Carson show, Uecker noted that, "Most people's bats said 'Powerized' down at the end. Mine said 'For Display Purposes Only'." It was Uecker who first stated, "The best way to catch a knuckle ball is to follow it until it stops rolling and then pick it up.

"I lacked speed," Uecker admitted in his book, *Catcher in the Wry*, published in 1982. "I had to compensate with a few tricks. One was to knock my hat off as I ran down the first base line to make it appear I was really moving."

Uecker has fond memories of the 1964 World Series, in which the Cardinals met the Yankees. The series lasted seven games, with the Cards winning. Uecker did not play an inning. Tim McCarver caught every game. McCarver batted .478, scored four runs, had five RBIs, and even stole a base. Uecker was hardly needed.

What Uecker remembers is an incident that took place before the first game. He was in the outfield shagging flies when he spotted a tuba unattended. There were several bands on the field to entertain the fans, and one of them had taken a break. Some of the musicians had left their instruments on the field. Uecker went over and picked up the big funnel-shaped instrument, draped it around his neck, and started catching fly balls with it.

Several hit the rim, leaving dents. Later the Cardinals received a bill for damages from the tuba's owner. That was as close as Uecker got to playing in the 1964 World Series.

The next year, Uecker was traded to Philadelphia, where he played for the Phillies for two years. In a game during the season of 1967, Uecker realized that the Phillies were no longer interested in him. He went to the plate as a pinch hitter, and when he looked at the third base coach for a sign, the coach turned his back on him. Sure enough, Uecker was traded to Atlanta soon after.

Uecker provided comic relief off the field as well as on it. Once, when he was with the Braves, the team plane was coming in for a landing. Just as the aircraft was about to touch down, a moment when many players get very tense, Uecker picked up the intercom microphone at the back of the plane and announced in crisp tones: "This is your captain speaking. Please remain seated and keep your seat belts fastened until the plane HAS HIT THE SIDE OF THE TERMINAL BUILDING and come to a complete stop.

"It was fun watching the blood leave their faces for a few seconds," Uecker said.

The one ability that Uecker had was the ability to laugh at himself and at a game that little kids can play pretty well. He turned that ability into a career after his retirement, becoming a broadcaster for the Milwaukee Brewers and ABC-TV's "Monday Night Baseball."

OUTFIELD: JIMMY PIERSALL, KEN HARRELSON, BABE HERMAN—
Of Jimmy Piersall, who had a well-deserved reputation for bizarre behavior, Casey Stengel once said, "He's great, but you gotta play him in a cage."

During a 17-year career in which he played for the Red Sox, Indians, Senators, Giants, and Angels, Piersall was always doing the unexpected. Once, after hitting a home run, he circled the bases running backwards. Another time, he slid safely into second base, then stood, drew a water pistol from his pocket, and squirted the umpire. "You're darn right I'm safe!" he declared. "It's the first call you've gotten right all day."

Piersall was playing center field for the California Angels at Yankee Stadium one afternoon when he pulled off one of his weirdest pranks. The Angels began shelling the Yankee pitcher, reaching him for eight runs by the fifth inning. Time after time, balls were drilled into the alley in left center, a long chase for the center fielder in those days before the outfield fence was moved when the Stadium was reconstructed. Piersall's tongue was hanging out from all the running.

There were no outs and the bases were loaded when manager Bill Rigney went out to the mound to talk to the pitcher. After a brief meeting, Rigney decided he would let the pitcher continue. He returned to the dugout and play was about to resume when suddenly the umpire yelled "Time!" There was nobody in center field.

A search was launched. Where was Piersall? Finally they found him. He was hiding behind the granite monuments dedicated to Babe Ruth and Gehrig near the wall in deep center field.

"Hey, I've got a wife and nine kids and I've been chasing balls all afternoon," said Piersall. "Someone's liable to get hurt. I'm not coming back until you get that guy off the mound."

Rigney shook his head in bewilderment. But he was saved the necessity of making a decision when the umpire informed him that he *had* to remove the pitcher. In the confusion, Rigney had gone to the mound a second time in the inning, a breach of the rules that made removal of the pitcher mandatory.

During the early 1980s, Piersall served as a broadcaster for the Chicago White Sox.

Piersall clowns with Disney's Goofy.

As Piersall's career was winding down, his role as one of baseball's prize flakes was taken over by Ken (Hawk) Harrelson. From 1963 through 1971, Harrelson played for four teams, the A's, Senators, Red Sox, and Indians.

While Harrelson didn't do outrageous things, he is important because some of his antics set new trends in baseball style and fashion. Harrelson, for example, was the first player to wear a glove when batting. Sometimes players of the 1950s would wear golf gloves in batting practice or spring training, but never during the regular season.

Harrelson started the fashion by accident. He liked to spend his days playing golf. One day during the 1964 season, when he felt sure he wasn't going to be in the lineup that night, Harrelson played 27 holes. All that club swinging left his left hand blistered and raw.

When he arrived at the ball park later in the day, Harrelson was stunned to find his name in the batting order. But how could he swing a bat with his left hand so mangled? His only solution was to wear his golf glove. Harrelson hit a homer that night. He never played without the glove again.

Other players began to wear golf gloves. Equipment manufacturers saw a chance to capitalize on a new product and began turning out batting gloves in a variety of sizes and styles.

"The major contribution of Harrelson," writer Leonard Koppett once observed, "was that he proved that a player didn't have to conform. He proved that you wouldn't embarrass yourself if you weren't like the next guy. It was part of the 1960s philosophy of 'do your own thing,' and he was the first baseball player to embody it."

Harrelson was the first player to wear sweat bands for the

wrists. "You don't realize how much you can sweat in Kansas City," he said.

Lampblack under the eyes to reduce the sun's glare was another of Harrelson's innovations. "I got it from playing football," he said.

Harrelson was also the first player to wear high stirrups, exposing most of the white sanitary socks beneath and showing little of the team colors. High stirrups, of course, are as prevalent today as batting helmets.

Harrelson deserves a niche in baseball history, not for these achievements, but for his role as baseball's first free agent. It happened in 1967, a season that the Hawk got into a dispute with Kansas City owner Charlie Finley. A newspaper quoted Harrelson as saying that Finley was "a menace to baseball."

Harrelson denied the statement (although he did admit to saying that Finley was "bad" for the game). Finley was so angry he released Harrelson in midseason, whereupon the Hawk began receiving offers from other teams. He soon signed with the Red Sox for a reported $75,000 bonus and a two-year contract worth $100,000. In Kansas City, Harrelson had been earning $13,000.

Harrelson surprised many people in 1971 by quitting baseball to try his hand at professional golf. "Why not?" he said. "I can belt the ball off the tee and putt like crazy. But as a ballplayer, I can't throw, I can't run or field well. I was the highest paid .240 hitter in all of baseball history."

Harrelson quickly demonstrated he was no Tom Watson as a golfer. Later, like Piersall, he became a baseball broadcaster. Harrelson's team was the Boston Red Sox.

Babe Herman, who played for the Brooklyn Dodgers in the late 1920s and, after that, several other teams, was a wacky player in the traditional sense. He started out as a first baseman. He could catch the ball all right, but when he threw it no one could be sure where it was going to go. As Kyle Crichton, writing in *Collier's* magazine, once observed, "Whenever Babe got hold of the ball, the players in both dugouts dropped down behind the concrete and hid, fans in all parts of the field cowered in fright, and the grounds keepers hastily locked the gates to keep the ball in the park."

The Dodgers had no wish to release Herman because he had a powerful bat, so manager Wilbert Robinson shifted him to the outfield. Not long after, a story began making the rounds that Herman had been hit on the head while trying to catch a fly ball. There was no truth to the story. A sportswriter predicted that Herman *would* get hit on the head if he didn't improve his fielding skills. Herman offered to bet the writer it would never happen.

"How about the shoulder?" said the writer. "Will you pay off on that?"

"Oh, no," said Herman. "Only the head. The shoulder doesn't count."

The time he doubled into a double play was the most famous of Herman's many wacky exploits. It happened in a game against the Braves in 1926. The bases were full when Herman came to bat—Chick Fewster was on first, Dazzy Vance on second, and Hank DeBerry on third. Herman drilled a long, high drive that caromed off the right field wall. DeBerry romped home with a run.

Vance and Fewster took off from second and first. Herman rounded first under a full head of steam and headed for second.

Vance turned the corner at third base, but then decided he could never make it home, and reversed his field and darted back for the bag.

Although a clown, Babe Herman was hailed for his powerful bat.

Fewster was pounding toward third from second. Herman, his head down and still charging, crossed second base and also set out for third. All three men went diving headfirst into third together.

The third baseman quickly tagged all three Dodgers. The umpire ruled the base belonged to Vance and that Fewster and Herman were out.

The Brooklyn team of this period was known as the Daffiness Boys. They were never daffier than the day they put three men on the same base.

PITCHER: DIZZY DEAN — A look back through baseball history confirms that pitchers have always excelled when it comes to nutty behavior. Pitcher nicknames are evidence of this. We have had Bo and Bobo, Dazzy and Goofy, and Dizzy and Daffy.

"Bo" was the nickname for Robert Belinsky who had a stormy eight-year career with five teams during the 1960s. Bo won only 28 games but, thanks to his love of bright lights, strong drink, big cars, and attractive women, was in the headlines frequently. "Bobo" was Louis Newsom. He won 211 games during his career. But he also lost a bundle, 222, in fact. He is the only 200-game winner in baseball to have lost more games than he won.

"Dazzy" was the nickname pinned on Clarence Vance, a teammate of Babe Herman's in the days of the Daffiness Boys of Brooklyn. "Goofy" was Yankee pitcher Vernon Gomez, also known as Lefty. He struck a match at home plate one overcast day to make sure superfast Bob Feller could see so as not to hit him.

"Dizzy" and "Daffy" were the nicknames of the famous Dean brothers of the 1930s, Jay Hanna (Dizzy) Dean and Paul Dee (Daffy) Dean. Besides their reputations as characters, they were the outstanding pitchers of their time. Dizzy won 20 or more games in four consecutive years for the Cardinals, and was the last National League pitcher to win 30 games; he was 30–7 in 1934.

Brother Paul twice won 19 games for the Cards. In 1934, the brothers had a combined total of 49 wins, pitching the Cardinals to the league championship, then winning all four games as St. Louis whipped Detroit in the World Series.

Their father was an Arkansas cotton picker and farmhand. Dizzy spent his boyhood doing manual labor in the cotton fields at fifty cents a day. He went only as far as fourth grade in school. As a teenager, it was found that he could throw a baseball with startling speed and make it do tricks.

He earned the name "Dizzy" in an exhibition game in which he was striking out White Sox batters one after another. He was confusing them. They were in a daze. He was a pitcher of dizziness. Somebody called him Dizzy, and the name stuck.

In 1934, Dizzy's brother Paul joined him as a member of the Cardinals. A baseball writer applied the nickname "Daffy" to Paul because it paired well with "Dizzy." The nickname "Dizzy" was a natural. Everybody called him Dizzy or Diz. But Daffy was never accepted by those who knew Paul. Dizzy was the comedian. Paul was his best audience.

Dizzy not only had speed and great control, he had enormous confidence. He would yell to a batter, "Can you hit a curve?" and then he'd blaze a curve right by him.

Before a St. Louis-Boston game one season, a friend bet Dean that he couldn't strike out Vince DiMaggio four times.

Dean agreed to the bet. "Let's make it twenty cents per strikeout," he said.

The first three times DiMaggio came to the plate, Dizzy struck him out. His fourth time at bat, DiMaggio fouled off the first pitch. He fouled off the second pitch high into the air just behind the plate. As Bruce Ogrodowski, the Cardinal catcher, camped

JAY HANNA (DIZZY) DEAN
ST. LOUIS (N.L.) 1932 1937
CHICAGO (N.L.) 1938 - 1941

ONE OF FOUR N.L. PITCHERS TO WIN 30 OR
MORE GAMES UNDER MODERN REGULATIONS.
PITCHED IN 1934 (ST.L.) 1938 (CHICAGO)
WORLD SERIES. LED LEAGUE IN STRIKEOUTS
1932-33-34-35. SINGLE GAME RECORD WITH
17, JULY 30, 1933. FIRST PITCHER TO MAKE
TWO HITS IN ONE INNING IN WORLD SERIES
MOST VALUABLE N.L. PLAYER IN 1934.

Dean is one of a small handfull of baseball flakes to have won election to the Hall of Fame.

under the ball, Dean rushed in from the mound yelling, "Drop it! Drop it! I gotta bet! I gotta fan him!"

The flustered Ogrodowski let the ball slip through his hands.

Dean returned to the mound and struck out DiMaggio on the next pitch. Besides the ball game, he had won eighty cents.

Dizzy was a tireless prankster. Once, on a blistering hot day in St. Louis, with the crowd sweltering, a wisp of smoke curled out of the Cardinal dugout. Dean, decked out in a heavy overcoat, was warming his hands over a fire he had built.

The Cardinals of this period were a rowdy, scrappy bunch, known as the Gashouse Gang. They often pulled off stunts together. One of their looniest involved Dean and teammates Pepper Martin and Rip Collins. Wearing overalls and painters' caps, the trio showed up one afternoon in the cocktail lounge of the hotel in Philadelphia where the team was staying. They set up a stepladder at one end of the room and started measuring. Dean, a pad in one hand, a pencil in the other, was the foreman. Martin and Collins called out measurements, and Dean jotted them down. The room emptied of customers within a few minutes. If the hotel manager hadn't appeared to protest, Dean and his co-workers would have repainted the room.

Dean had five brilliant seasons with the Cardinals. Then, at 26, a crippling injury cut him down. A line drive off the bat of Earl Averill in the 1937 All-Star game struck him on the left foot, breaking his big toe. Dean tried to pitch too soon after the injury and, throwing unnaturally, damaged muscles in his left shoulder. His arm was never the same again.

After his retirement from baseball, Dean became a broadcaster on the "Game of the Week" telecasts. He was like no other broadcaster before or since in his treatment of the English language; he brutalized it.

"Marion throwed Reiser out at the plate," Dean would say.

"Slaughter slud safe into second," was another Dean-ism.

"Airs" was a term Dean used frequently, as in "No hits, no runs, no airs."

He used "swang" as either the present or past tense of the verb "swing."

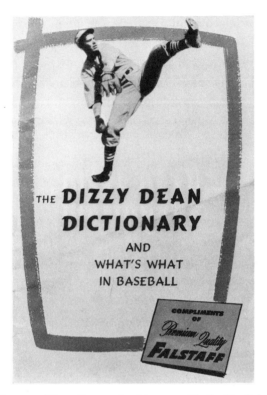

THE DIZZY DEAN DICTIONARY

AND
WHAT'S WHAT
IN BASEBALL

COMPLIMENTS
OF
Premium Quality
FALSTAFF

As a broadcaster, Dizzy Dean raised havoc with the English language. His sponsor published a dictionary of his words and phrases.

English teachers protested Dean's abuse of the language, including his frequent use of the word "ain't." They said his broadcasts were having a bad influence on students.

Dean was quick to answer his critics. "Maybe I am butcherin' up the English language a little," he said. "Well, all I gotta say is when me and my brother and Pa was pickin' cotton in Arkansas, we didn't have no chance to go to school much. I'm glad that kids today are gettin' that chance."

MANAGER: CASEY STENGEL—At the age of 58, when most managers have long-since retired, Casey Stengel embarked upon an exceptional career as manager of the New York Yankees. He established a record of winning ten American League pennants and seven world championships in twelve years. Another record of Casey's was winning five world championships in a row, from 1949 to 1954.

Stengel was a well-known figure in New York baseball, laughing, joking, and double-talking with the press. With his players, however, he could be sarcastic and aloof.

He created his own language—Stengelese. It added to his comic image.

One of Stengel's most notable performances occurred in 1958 when he was called upon to testify during the U.S. Senate hearings on antitrust and monopoly.

Senator Estes Kefauver asked Stengel: "Will you give us very briefly your background and your views on this legislation?"

This was Stengel's answer: "Well, I started in professional ball in 1912. I have been in professional ball for 48 years and have been employed by numerous ball clubs in the major and minor leagues . . . How could you transfer a ball club when you did not have a highway? How could you transfer a ball club when the railroads then would take you to a town you got off and then you had to wait and sit up five hours to go to another ball club? How could you run baseball then without night ball? You had to have night ball to improve the proceeds, to pay larger salaries, and I went to work the first year I recieved $135 a month. I thought that was amazing. I had to put away money to go to dental college. I found out it was no better in dentistry. I stayed in baseball. Any other questions you would like to ask me?"

Stengel's career in baseball began in 1912, when he played for the New York Giants.

That was Stengelese.

Stengel had a reputation as a buffoon long before he signed to manage the Yankees. He managed the Boston Bees in 1939. In a game against the New York Giants at the Polo Grounds, Boston was trailing and Stengel wanted the umpires to stop the game on account of darkness. The umpires refused, whereupon Casey Stengel emerged from the dugout carrying a railroad lantern. "Don't want the trains to run over me in this here darkness," he said.

The next day it rained. Again Casey wanted the umpires to halt play. Again they said no. This time Casey came out of the dugout with an umbrella and wearing a raincoat and galoshes.

Earlier, when he was a player, Casey pulled off a stunt that has become legendary. He was an outfielder for the Brooklyn Dodgers at the time. The fans were so upset with his play that they started giving him the "bird," that is, hooting and jeering at him.

Casey caught a sparrow in the outfield and secreted it under his cap. During his last time at bat of the day, Casey, with an exaggerated flourish, doffed his cap to the fans—thus giving them the bird.

Stengel managed the New York Mets from 1962, the year the team was founded, until 1965. The Mets were so inept they were laughed at, and Stengel added to his reputation as a clown during this period.

Right up until his departure from baseball at the age of 75, Stengel was a fast man with a quip. Once, when his future as a manager was a bit clouded, reporters asked him, "Will you be back? What about next year?"

"What do I know about next year?" Stengel said in reply. "People my age are dead next year."

Index

144

145